AMERICAN
MILITARISM

AMERICAN MILITARISM

THE HENRY L. STIMSON LECTURES, 2018

THE MACMILLAN CENTER,
YALE UNIVERSITY

WILLIAM R. POLK

Panda Press

First Panda Press Edition, 2018
Published in the United States by Panda Press

The Library of Congress has catalogued this edition as follows:
Polk, William Roe 1929-
American Militarism by William R. Polk, 1st edition
ISBN: 978-0-9829340-6-7

Editor: Milbry Polk
Design: Mary Tiegreen

TABLE OF CONTENTS

Introduction by
Professor Ian Shapiro

PROFESSOR OF POLITICAL SCIENCE AND
DIRECTOR OF THE MACMILLAN CENTER,
YALE UNIVERSITY

Welcome to the Whitney and Betty MacMillan Center for International and Area Studies at Yale. I am Ian Shapiro, Professor of Political Science and Director of the MacMillan Center of Yale University. We are delighted to host William R. Polk as this year's Henry L. Stimson Lecturer.

The funding for this lecture series comes from an anonymous donor, in honor of Henry L. Stimson, Yale College 1889, an attorney and statesman whose government service culminated with his tenure as secretary of war during World War II.

Since 1998, the MacMillan Center and the Yale University Press have collaborated to bring distinguished diplomats and foreign policy experts to the Center to lecture on their books that are published by the Yale Press. Previous Stimson Lectures have included "Political Order in Changing Societies" by Samuel P. Huntington; "Financial Crises in Emerging Markets" by Alexandre Lamfalussy; "Arms and Influence" by

Thomas C. Schelling; "The Arab Center: The Promise of Moderation" by Ambassador Marwan Muasher; "Beyond the Democratic Maze" by John Dunn; "What Happened to National Liberation" by Michael Walzer; "The Imprint of Congress," by David Mayhew; "FDR's Third Hundred Days" by Susan Dunn; and "Liberal Ideals & International Realities" by John J. Mearsheimer.

William Polk is a veteran foreign policy consultant, author, and professor. Mr. Polk taught history and Arabic language and literature and helped to found the Center for Middle Eastern Studies at Harvard University from 1955 until 1961, when President Kennedy appointed him the Member of the Policy Planning Council responsible for the Middle East, Central Asia and much of Africa. During the Cuban Missile Crisis, he served as one of three members of the Crisis Management Committee. During this period, he was asked to become Deputy Commissioner General of the United Nations Relief and Works Agency for Palestine Refugees in the Near East (UNRWA).

In 1965, Mr. Polk resigned from government service to become Professor of History at the University of Chicago. There he established the Center for Middle Eastern Studies and was a founding director of the American Middle Eastern Studies Association. In 1967, he became the founding director (later President) of the Adlai Stevenson Institute of International Affairs which, among other ventures, hosted the 20th Pugwash Conference on nuclear weapons and did much of the planning for the United Nations Environment Program.

Mr. Polk was called back to the White House briefly during the 1967 Middle Eastern war to write a draft peace treaty and to act as assistant to the former Director of the National Security Council and then the President's special assistant, McGeorge Bundy, who incidentally gave these lectures some years ago. In 1970, at the request of Israeli Prime Minister Golda Meir, he successfully negotiated with President Nasser of Egypt a ceasefire on the Suez Canal.

He is the author of many books on world affairs, including The United States and the Arab World; The Elusive Peace, the Middle East in the Twentieth Century; Understanding Iraq; Out of Iraq (with Senator George McGovern); Understanding Iran; Violent Politics: A History of Insurgency and Terrorism; Neighbors and Strangers: The Fundamentals of Foreign Affairs; Humpty Dumpty: The Fate of Regime Change; and Distant Thunder: Reflections on the Dangers of Our Times. His latest work, published by the Yale University Press, is titled Crusade and Jihad: The Thousand-Year War Between the Muslim World and the Global North.

A number of his articles have appeared in Foreign Affairs, The Atlantic, Harpers, The Bulletin of the

Atomic Scientists, and Le Monde Diplomatique.

Mr. Polk is here to give three lectures on "American Militarism." Today is the first of the three, and it's titled "How It All Began: How American Colonialism and Altruism Shaped Americans' Image of Ourselves and Set a Pattern of Foreign Policy." His next lecture will be on Monday and titled "Dealing with Militarism." Wednesday's lecture will be entitled "A Warring People: What We Have Tried to Enhance the Chances of Our Achieving Affordable World Security."

I hope you will join us again for both of them.I am delighted to introduce William Polk.

HOW IT ALL BEGAN:
AMERICANS LEARN ABOUT WAR

Professor Shapiro, Professor Monteiro, colleagues and friends, I am delighted to be with you here at Yale to give the lectures in honor of Henry L. Stimson; so, in beginning, I tip my hat to him. Mr. Stimson, in a long and distinguished career served as Secretary of War, State and once again of War. He oversaw the rise of the American military. During his first assignment in 1911, the US had military forces numbering about 145 thousand men; during the Second World War, he oversaw forces that aggregated about 13 million men and women.

As I will emphasize, it was the experience that Mr. Stimson exemplified that not only marked our government but did much to shape the society as we now know it. As he reflected over his experience, he wrote that "Foreign affairs are now our most intimate domestic concern. All men, good or bad, are now our neighbors. All ideas dwell among us."

What I want to discuss with you are three interlocking topics that arose from but were not covered in my book, Crusade and Jihad, that the Yale University Press has just published.

In that book, I focused on international affairs—what the imperialists of the North (China and Russia in Asia; Western Europe and England in Africa and Asia and eventually America in the Philippines) did to the peoples

1

of the South (particularly to the Muslim societies of Africa and Asia). I also dealt there with how those societies have reacted.

Thus, I lay out the causes and the courses of many of the dangers and conflicts that are such a prominent feature of our time. We are the legatees of imperialism and colonialism and the struggle against them.

I believe, and here argue, that what we divide into the separate categories of international affairs and domestic affairs are just the two sides of the same coin.

But, we rarely think of them in that way. Rather we treat them, academically, in government and in the media— indeed, in our individual thoughts—as almost unrelated.

I believe this division has dangerous, indeed sometimes disastrous, consequences and obscures what we need to understand in our quest for what I have called "affordable world security."

Thus, I begin by showing how America and Americans were affected and our national "character" was largely formed by the same forces—colonialism, imperialism and war that have impacted so strongly on Europeans, Africans and Asians.

So, having dealt with the international aspects of our quest for the security that would enable us to lead a healthy, happy and harmonious life, in Crusade and Jihad, I turn to the other side of the same coin, the domestic side.

In each of my three discussions with you, I propose to focus on an aspect of national experience. And I will allude where appropriate to the parallels of our experience, the American experience, with the experiences of other peoples.

I deeply believe that if we are to move meaningfully and in a timely fashion toward the peace and security we all want for ourselves and our children, we need, first of all, to acquire a sensitive and realistic view of ourselves and those with whom we must share our Earth. We need to know what we did, how our actions affected others and how they were seen by those upon whom they impacted.

In my talk today, I look at the flip side of Mr. Stimson's comment to say that our domestic experience, the colonization of America, where we dealt with the native Americans, has been formative of our most significant ventures into foreign relations.

I will point out that the great process of colonization was essentially the same throughout the world—that indeed our domestic experience of colonialism led us into our first major foreign venture, the conquest and rule of the Philippines. I will emphasize that there is a unity of world history that we cannot afford to overlook. Or, as Mr. Stimson put it, "All men, good or bad, are now our neighbors. All ideas dwell among us." We sense them both in militarism and in altruism.

In my second talk, on Monday, I will discuss how those who laid out the "contract"—the Constitution that binds us together as a nation—worried about and tried to protect us from the dangers of militarism and draining, disruptive and demeaning warfare and how and wby we have wandered from their wise prescriptions into unending warfare.

Finally, in my third talk, this coming Wednesday, I pick up where I left off the discussion of our relations with the native Americans, colonialism and our first imperial venture and show how we have carried to almost the whole world strategies and tactics we applied in domestic affairs.

Clearly, the reciprocal is also true. We cannot avoid the fact that we live in a world increasingly interconnected instead of what in my youth almost everyone I knew thought that we could isolate ourselves beyond the great oceans and stand aloof from the rest of humanity.

I have laughed, as you probably also have, at the notion that the flutter of a butterfly's wing in Brazil can flow through, be magnified by and be carried along through various climates to whip up a tornado in Texas. But, that is nearly the world of today and surely will be the world of our grandchildren.

So, in my third talk, I zero in on our plans, hopes and actions to show how we have carried to almost the whole world strategies and tactics we applied in domestic affairs and also to show how the beat of the butterfly wings or the more insistent repetition of banishment, boycott and bombing has shaped our daily lives and the daily lives of people all over the world.

As journalists have taught us to disclose, I must mention that I have been personally involved in some of the issues I will discuss. Where that is relevant, I will reveal my actions and thoughts.

There is much to discuss and little time so I ask your indulgence. I will endeavor to be both brief and provocative. Now, let me get to work!

*   *   *

As a historian, I have learned to respect folk wisdom which is often embodied in fairy tales so I begin there.

You all will remember Snow White's Magic Mirror into which the queen gazed to see who is "the fairest of all." For years, she saw what she wanted to see, and the mirror reassured her. She was fairest of all. We do the same. The image we see in our school text books, in the pronouncements of our politicians and in the media— our magic mirrors—is always a beautiful, bountiful and benevolent America. Like the Snow White's stepmother, most of us would like to stop there.

But, in the fairy tale, the mirror did not stop there. Ours has stopped on that note. We are reassured constantly that we are unique, a people apart from all others, certainly the fairest of all.

But, let us pretend that our magical mirror is also a one-way window through which others can see us. We know that they see a different image.

To see both—what we see and what others see—is one of the great challenge we face today. We cannot afford to see only our side. So in my analysis, I will attempt to keep in view both what We see and what Others see.

Doing so is not easy and is sometimes even painful, but it is not the only challenge. It is not just our image that counts. In our conduct, we Americans present a complex, often baffling, combination of beauty and ugliness, of violence and altruism, of war and peace.

As the popular historian Arthur Schlesinger wrote, "The American character is indeed filled with contradiction and paradox." We are not easy to understand even for ourselves and we baffle most others.

At no time in our history was this more true than at the beginning. So it should be easier for us to comprehend —and be willing to accept—if we focus on the remote past. After all, most of us are not in any sense responsible for what ancestors or others then did. We are a people composed of waves of immigrants, so increasing numbers of us are not related except by historical memory and cultural implants to the early Americans. But, even so, getting a clear view of the past is not easy.

We actually don't know much about the beginning of our national experience. Even in geography, the story is complex. What we know anchors the beginning far away from where most of us would put it.

In our schoolbooks, we often get a picture that focuses just on the English migration. We sometimes forget that much of what became the United States was colonized by Spain. And even those who know most about Spain often brush over Spain's experience in colonialism. Mexico and Peru figure in text books as the sources of gold, silver and romance. The glorious Spanish empire merged with and absorbed the less warlike empires of the Incas and Aztecs. But, as we read more carefully, we see that the Spaniards arrived knowing what to do. They had learned about colonialism already in Europe by dispossessing and following abroad their Muslim and Jewish fellow inhabitants and in exterminating the Guanche natives of the Canary Islands.

What they learned in the Canaries, they applied to the native populations of the Caribbean. There, as Bartolomé de las Casas told us, they engaged in genocide. The record of Spanish colonialism there and in what became the south of our country was a tale of horror. And they recorded it for us to read.

In contrast to what we can learn in the fulsome Spanish records, we don't know much our English beginnings and much of what we tell ourselves is myth. Many of us would like to date our ancestors to the Mayflower—that is not quite an impossible claim because there were quite a few ships of that name. So having ancestors who "came over on the Mayflower" is possible, but not very meaningful.

And the result was at least geographically accidental.

Those who sailed aboard the Mayflower never intended to reach your shores here in New England. They were trying to get to what became Virginia. Had the Mayflower reached there, the society we associate with it—of pious pilgrims sounding the call to liberty abroad but enforcing Old Testament laws at home—probably would have left a very different legacy for us.

But they left us one very important legacy even before they landed. While they were still at sea, the passengers on the Mayflower gave us one of the first major documents of our history, the Mayflower Compact. By signing the Compact, the refugees declared themselves to be "a civil Body Politick" and gave themselves power to enact laws "for the general Good of the Colony." Thus, although they prudently affirmed their loyalty to "our dread Sovereign Lord, King James," they declared themselves a self-governing society. Thus, they set a precedent for the Constitution that emerged 167 years later.

Then, perhaps unknowingly they also set out the elements of one of our enduring myths, Thanksgiving.

We have all grown up on the fairy tale of the happy Pilgrims sharing Thanksgiving with the loving Indians.

The reality was quite different.

The earliest immigrants to the New World were refugees. Some were escaping religious oppression while others were looking back over their shoulders at the savage events we know as the Wars of Religion when European Christians were massacring one another for even slight doctrinal differences.

Logically, the refugees on the various Mayflowers should have been among the most tolerant of societies: they had experienced and only narrowly escaped the horror of intolerance. But, as we know, we are seldom shaped by logic. History teaches us that we are more influenced by our enemies than by our ideals or even by our friends. Often we forget enemies, ideals and friends altogether.

The colonists did. As they looked forward, they focused on improving their lives. They had left Europe as religious refugees but came to America as what we call economic refugees. To the early immigrants, the colonists, that meant acquiring land.

To get land, as other colonists from England, France, Russia and China, were then doing and would continue to do in the Americas, Africa and Asia, they had to dispossess the natives who were occupying it.

In short, colonialism is marked by a unity in American and Afro-Asian history that most historians specializing in each separate area tend to overlook.

Seeing a different image in the magic mirror, in telling ourselves about American history, we like to focus on our benevolence. What we were doing was right. We cared no more for the Indians than the wicked queen cared about the scullery maid, "Snow White." She did not count and neither did they. Indians were just animals. We would like to believe that what we were doing was very different from what others were doing in Africa and Asia. But colonialism was everywhere similar in methods and objectives.

The English did not need Spain's tutelage. They had already learned about colonialism in Ireland where they sometimes shot natives for sport. They regarded the Irish just as the Spaniards had regarded the Guanche of the Canary Islands—as slightly advanced animals. The major difference was that there were too many Irish to exterminate whereas the Spaniards could—and did —exterminate the Gaunche. Both the Spaniards and the English were determined to get the one significant resource of the natives, their land. In Ireland, the English took the best land for themselves, planted colonies of their own subjects (including Scottish lowlanders), enforced a policy that led often to starvation of the Irish and built a wall—the pale—to keep the surviving natives at bay.

What the English did would be also done by the Russians with the Jews and the Turkish peoples of Central Asia and the Dutch with their Indonesians and the Belgians with the Congolese.

Colonialism knew no frontiers.

So what the colonists did in America was common practice and would mark the American experience for generations.

What distinguished American colonialism was not the degree of violence. That was common everywhere colonialism was practiced. What distinguished American colonialism was the combination of war and the proclamation of idealism.

Idealism was the message the Pilgrims prolaimed.

Just as John Winthrop was about to go ashore just up the coast from here in what became Massachusetts in June 1630, he addressed his band of pilgrim refugees with a summation of their task—"we shall be as a city on a hill…A modell of Christian Charity." He said. Christian charity did not, of course, extend to non-Christians and certainly not to natives.

But the message, at least in the form Winthrop proclaimed it, came in part at least the words of the natives. His "modell" was drawn from the dispossessed Natik tribesmen in whose language Massachusetts meant "the people of the high hill."

It was the Indians' high hill that was to become the Puritans' city, Boston, from which Indians were to be excluded.

And, from their first "high hill," the colonists ventured forth to other hills and other farm lands, driving out or massacring or selling into slavery their inhabitants.

As they did, the native Americans began to resist. War followed raid and counterattack led to massacre.

Most encounters were small, because the Indian societies were often small. Few left records. So what we have tended to see is only the image reflected on our side of the mirror.

But we have enough records to show that the early history of the New World is a chronicle of ethnic cleansing.

Here in Connecticut on the Mystic river, the Pequot War of 1636-1637 was typical of many encounters to follow. In it upwards of 700 Indians were killed and many more were sold as slaves to work in Bermuda. Scores, indeed hundreds, of other battles followed.

As the British and French did in the "other India," the Asian India, our ancestors incited rival Indian nations to destroy or conquer one another. In the French and Indian War, just before the Revolution, it was the Algonquians against the Iroquois.

In both New England "India" and Asian India it was easy to get the natives to destroy one another. Each society was alien to its neighbors, spoke different languages or dialects, had incompatible customs and worshiped other gods. Therefore, as in the "other" India, where Hindus could be encouraged to fight Muslims and little principalities could be turned against their neighbors, each native society could be used against others. Inciting war among them became the accepted tactic of imperialism.

But, over time, the British overlords of the American colonists found these continual wars expensive and disruptive and expensive. When strategy required it, regular British troops could be used. But often strategy did not require it. However, when used sporadically by small groups of land-hungry adventurers, often made up of Scotch-Irish émigrés whom the British regarded as virtual outlaws, the British found the restless moves into Indian lands inconvenient and costly. So, in 1763 the British tried to call a halt. They tried to interdict colonists' moves out into Indian lands.

But geography was against the British. They lacked the means to stop the flow. The frontier moved inexorably westward as little groups of Europeans hacked homesteads out of the wilderness or seized lands the Indians had already cleared.

Our school books tell us of the quest for liberty in the American Revolution—it was a real quest and the books are right as far as they go—but the British attempt to rescind illegal grabs of Indian lands in 1774 was one of the "oppressions" that incited the American Revolution.

Up to the actual outbreak of war with Britain, even our great hero George Washington sought to find and acquire fertile land more than independence from England, As he rode into Indian lands, he kept a sharp look out for lands the Indians had already cleared which he could acquire—and he acquired a lot—while at the same time he excoriated "Land Jobbers, Speculators…[and] scatter'd settlers…"

As the Revolutionary war broke out, Washington was not concerned with protecting Indian rights. He was worried about the ability of Indians to fight back or help the British. To the degree that he worried out the Indians, what bothered him was the cost of warfare. That is, the method of taking their land from them. There was no question of leaving the Indians their lands but, he wrote, "there is nothing to be obtained by an Indian war but the soil they live on and this can be had by purchase at less expence, and without that bloodshed…" In short, he was an enlightened colonist. So were nearly all of the Revolution's leaders including Benjamin Franklin who was a large-scale dealer in Indian land.

The first government that was set up to win independence for white America, the Confederation, was too weak to enforce a policy such as Washington (and the British rulers had) advocated. The Continental Congress had no more success in stopping the settlers and the speculators than the British had had. Indeed, the new state needed Indian lands since, following the Revolution, veterans— including members of my family—were paid off in newly seized Indian lands. So, engagements and expulsions followed.

When the expulsions accomplished their purpose, or where further engagements were too costly, a pause could be made by a temporary ceasefire or a treaty. But these treaties were merely stages in a Westward march.

The first treaty was made during the Revolutionary war (with the Delawares) in 1778 and the last was signed, almost a century later, with the Nez Perces in 1868. Between those dates 367 treaties with Indian societies were ratified by the Federal government. These treaties were just intervals of calm among the storms of conflict.

In 1788, Mr. Stimson's predecessor as Secretary of War, Henry Knox, observed to Congress that the white settlers "have frequently committed the most unprovoked and direct outrages against the Cherokee Indians [in] open violation of the treaty of peace made by the United States…to such a height as to amount to an actual although informal war…[and] have so flagitiously stained the American name."

Even denounced by such a senior official and even where shown to be a violation not only of honor but even of concrete national interests, the colonization system lingered on. Indeed, from the Indian side of the magic mirror, it became much worse. The major menace to the Indians was not the Federal Government, which, like Britain before the Revolution, was mainly interested in cutting the cost of maintain minimal public security. The almost daily threat to the Indians arose from the governments and militias of the former colonies that had become states and particularly from the new states along the Mississippi frontier. Their attitudes, policies and actions were driven by individuals, families and small groups that fought their ways down the three wagon roads that pierced the hundred miles of mountains that formed the barrier between the coastal settlements what contemporaries thought of as the Wilderness.

These settlers were wild, restless people, often Scotch-Irish. That is how the British thought of them and that is how the already established, more civilized and mainly English colonists on the coast regarded them. There were not civilized white men but savages, just "white Indians." As a contemporary (and horrified) Anglican missionary described them, "they expose themselves often quite naked, without Ceremony—Rubbing themselves and the Hair with Bears Oil and tying it up behind in a bunch like the Indians."

Not just in appearance but in fighting they borrowed from the Indians, but they were better armed and usually outnumbered the Indians. They won each fight. Step by step they drove into Indian lands. Their footprints deliniated the America to become.

As our great nineteenth-century American historian Henry Adams wrote in what has been called his "unread masterpiece," *The History of the United States of America*, there was an unconscious or at least unplanned strategy of conquest. "The people of the old thirteen States, along the Atlantic seaboard sent westward a wedge-shaped mass of nearly half a million people... [that] nearly split the Indian country in haves."

Few Americans today remember even the names of Indian societies—the still largely nomadic Wyandottes and Shawanese, Miamis and Kickapoos of the north and, the Creeks, Cherokees, Chickasaws, and Choctaws of the south. The northerners were still largely nomadic, but the southern Indians were sedentary. Even so enlightened a man as Henry Adams apparently did not realize that they had settled into agricultural and urban societies that were duplicates of the English colonies that had become states. Dealing with the former colonies, the Federal government took the word "state" in its literal meaning.

Each state took for itself the attribute of sovereignty: except in subjects set apart for the Federal government, each did what it could in in pursuit of its own interests. But, by the Constitution, the Federal government retained specified powers of which one was relations with foreign powers. The treaties it contracted became overriding laws to which the states were bound. One was the Treaty of Ghent that ended the war of 1812. In that treaty, the United States, that is the Federal Government, had bound itself to return all the territories taken from what were then called the five civilized tribes, the Creeks, Cherokees, Choctaws, Chickasaws and Seminoles. That was the law, but both state officials and private citizens, simply ignored the treaty.

When Andrew Jackson led military campaigns against the southern Indians, he practiced what all colonial armies did—as in the Russian campaign against the Chechens, the Chinese campaign against the Zungarians and the French campaign against the Algerians—he practiced virtual genocide to clear the land.

Then when he became president, Jackson introduced a

new element. We would today call it the "good cop, bad cop" ploy.

If the Indians did not go along with his (the Federal or good cop) policy, they would be faced with the claims —and the military forces—of the bad cops (the states, Georgia, Alabama and Mississippi). each of which claimed jurisdiction and would be given freedom to act under "their sovereign character."

Sovereign character, while today the phrase sounds recondite, it was then a key political issue. Who or what were the Indians? While obviously they were societies, were they also "states" in the sense that Britain and France were states with a position, however vague, in the Law of Nations? The issue came to focus on the Cherokees.

Cherokees had lived in what became southeastern United States for time out of mind of man; the Spanish Conquistador Hernando de Soto encountered them in 1542; English colonists in the Carolinas traded with them from at least 1673; in 1711 they became allies of the British in fighting another Indian people, the Tuscaroras. And, they signed a peace treaty with the United States in 1785 and another in 1791. Around 1800 they were thought to possess 53,000 square miles of land in Tennessee, North Carolina, Georgia and Alabama. That was their homeland and the cause of their tragedy.

Contemporaries and later historians usually blame Jackson for the tragedy, but its terms were set long before

Jackson became President. Even Thomas Jefferson, before his term as president, began to think about "removing" the Indians so that whites could take over their lands. He thought that might be done more or less peacefully. What he proposed was to so corrupt their leaders that, for private gain, they would sell what was the communal or tribal property on which their fellow tribesmen lived. Then in 1817, pressed by Georgia, President Monroe offered the Cherokees a deal. In the "Treaty of the Cherokee Agency" he proposed an acre for acre land swap: One acre east of the Mississippi for one acre west of the river.

The Cherokees, naturally, were not attracted by the proposal. They or their ancestors had cleared land and built houses and assembled into towns. To move they would have had to start all over again in an unknown but almost certainly hostile land. And they would have had to become colonists themselves and drive out the people who lived on the western lands in a new round of wars. Finally, they had come to regard themselves as Native Americans, far more American in culture than the "White Indians." They wanted to stay put and be accepted as fellow citizens.

Disturbing to the whites, over the previous century, they had "evolved." Were they still "savages" or people like the whites? Many had taken English names, created schools similar to those opened by the white colonists in the settled coastal districts, developed civic institutions much like the whites, and long before the Revolution, already in the 1740s, they had settled down as farmers.

Then, as they gradually came to see what was in store for them—the loss of their homeland—the Cherokee tribal government (which had been patterned on the state governments) passed a law in 1819 prohibiting any further cessation of land. That act proved that they, like the Puritans on the Mayflower and our Founding Fathers, could create a political society. Then, in 1827, Cherokee delegates met, as our Founding Fathers had done, forty years before, and adopted a constitution modeled on the one our Founding Fathers had written.

So, were they by the terms of the law of the United States a sovereign state, as they claimed to be? The United States government seemed to agree that they were by entering into treaty relationship with them. Or were they colonies, as the states proclaimed? Or some other sort of society?

The question forced the Supreme Court—or, rather, the Cherokees tried to force it—into the controversy.

Under the leadership of Chief Justice John Marshall, the Court made two historic decisions. In the first, in 1831, *Cherokee Nation vs Georgia,* the justices were divided. Justice Marshall, who was not himself a lawyer, wrote for the majority that the Cherokees were not a sovereign foreign nation but were a "domestic dependent nation" and could not address the Supreme Court. So, under his leadership, the Court refused to hear their case.

One of Marshall's colleagues went further. He maintained that the Cherokees were not a society at all but "nothing more than wandering hordes…having neither rules nor government" while two other justices opined that having made treaties with them, the Federal government had already ruled that they were indeed states.

For my purposes here, what was also significant was that the Court was not aware of the similarity between what was happening in America and in Asia and Africa as powerful nation-states overwhelmed weak societies. On behalf of the Court, Marshall wrote that "The condition of the Indians in relation to the United States is, perhaps, unlike that of any other two people in existence…[it] marked by peculiar and cardinal distinctions which exist nowhere else." But, of course the "peculiar" relationship of the colonized to the colonizers existed throughout the colonial world. Ughurs, Chechens, Tatars, Indonesians, Bengalis, Berbers, Arabs, Sudanese, and other colonial people were unknown to John Marshall, but their experiences would have been understood by the Cherokees.

And a year later, Marshall changed his mind.

In a case known as *Worcester vs Georgia,* the Court in effect accepted that the Cherokees were a sovereign state. Therefore, Georgia had no right to enforce state laws in Cherokee territory and the Indian Removal Act was invalid, illegal. unconstitutional and in violation of previous treaties.

Associate Justice Joseph Story, who had dissented in the first case, was delighted. Privately, he wrote to a friend,

"Thanks be to God, the Court can wash their hands clean of the iniquity of oppressing the Indians and disregarding their rights."

Well, not quite so fast. President Jackson was unmoved. On learning of the verdict, he was alleged to have said, "John Marshall has made his decision; now let him enforce it."

Whether or not those were his exact words, decisions made by the Court to protect the Indians were whistling against the wind. The very concept of the rule of law was then still very weak in America. Jackson spoke for "the people"—the still poor and land hungry settlers on the frontier, while Justice Marshall spoke for the already established and relatively wealthy inhabitants of the coastal areas of America. Jackson was a Democrat — which he interpreted to mean a populist—while Marshall was a Federalist. Those divisions would remain powerful and would often rally Americans as they still do today.

Regardless of the Supreme Court, Indian removal continued. And it became increasingly violent. The Cherokees and other Indians were driven across the Mississippi along what became known as the Trail of Tears. Of the 15,000 men, women and children who were driven out of their homes toward what is now Oklahoma, 4,000 died.

The horror of their forced migration was witnessed and described by a young French visitor to America. What Alexis de Tocqueville then observed on Indian removal came back to haunt him in later life when, as a member of the French National Assembly, he would warn his colleagues of the price to be paid for French colonialism in Algeria. He cut to the quick of colonialism when he wrote, "The social tie, which distress had long since weakened, is then dissolved; they [the inhabitants] have no longer a country, and soon they will not be a people; their very families are obliterated, their common name is forgotten; their language perishes; and all traces of their origin disappear."

Whereas in Africa and Asia, cultural genocide—what we might call ethnocide—was a policy deliberately orchestrated by French, Chinese, Russian, British and other governments, in America it was generally a haphazard process, carried out by Federal and State governments, companies and individuals, speculators and religious societies. But, gradually, the program was set and administered, as it was in Africa and Asia, by Federal or Central governments.

In 1873, the Federal Commissioner of Indian affairs wrote that the United States has "in theory over sixty-five independent nations within our borders" with whom the Federal government had "entered into treaty relations as being sovereign peoples" but, he noted, "it rules them as wards of the Government."

As wards of the Government, the Indians were to be kept apart from ordinary—that is to say, White—citizens.

We can date the process to Colonial Massachusetts,

where recently defeated Indians were moved into what were called Praying Towns where they could be kept under watch while they were being "improved."

That experience may be taken as the ancestor of the later policy of moving Indians into reservations that performed some of the functions of the Ghettos that had enclosed the Jews in medieval Europe and apartheid "reservations" in Africa.

By 1890, there were 162 Indian reservations in America. In them Indians were denationalized, as the blacks had been, and jumbled together despite differences in culture or even language. Theoretically, as wards of the Federal government with limited obligations and privileges, they were being prepared for citizenship. But, effectively, they were removed from American society. As the Congressionally appointed Indian Peace Commission noted, when the lands of the Indian are taken, the Indian himself is "lost sight of."

Again a parallel from domestic to international affairs. At the end of the First World War the "Powers" used the League of Nations as "cover" for the continuation of the colonial system in Africa and Asia. Under the title "mandates," colonies kept the inhabitants as "wards" while they were to be made into usable copies of Europeans. Many of the colonial or mandated peoples also felt that they were "lost sight of."

And like the Indians, many resisted. Their suppression and their resistance and its consequences will be a theme of my third lecture.

The last Indian-American war was in 1898. But memory of the centuries of struggle became part of the mythology of America and was to be the favorite subject in that great American "university," the movies. Let me confess, I learned my first history from the movies.

As a boy riding fences on my Father's ranch in Texas, it never occurred to me that only about half a century before, there were no fences and that my Father's ranch was Comanche territory. Nobody I knew, knew much or indeed anything about the Comanches, not even their correct name.

But, from the movies, I knew at least the name of the Apache chief Geronimo. The movies taught me that he was a vicious terrorist, tomahawk in hand, ready to scalp men, women and children. Scalping! How horrible. The very essence of terrorism. Even our worst enemies today would not practice it.

But, I did not know and certainly would not have believed that Texas and other state governments, including Connecticut, offered bounties for Indian scalps. (And so created a market for terrorism!) Unthinkable! The good guys were the Texas Rangers and the US cavalry.

As a child, I played cowboys and Indians with my young friends. We knew that "the only good Indian is a dead Indian." None of us wanted to be Indians. And even in our games, they always lost. My "magic mirror" reflected only white faces.   We were the "fairest of all."   The face I saw as a young cowboy was as a member of Warring America.

*   *   *

Here I pick up the second theme in our national character, the desire to do good.

Governor John Winthrop borrowed the theme, as he did all the regulations of his regime, from the Bible. While the edicts and social conventions of his community were largely drawn from the Old Testament and were draconian—complete with hangings, burnings and stonings to death—he cast his wider aspirations in the terms of the New Testament.

From Matthew 5, as the great English Biblical scholar William Tyndale rescued it from the Greek and put it into the memorable English we know as the King James version of the Bible, Winthrop drew his most famous proclamation:

> "Ye are the light of the world. A city that is set on a hill cannot be hid.

> "Neither do men light a candle, and put it under a bushel, but on a candlestick; and it giveth light until all that are in the house.

> "Let your light so shine before men that they may see your good works and glorify your Father which is in Heaven."

As I have pointed out, the light did not shine for Massachusetts's Indian neighbors. When one of Winthrop's followers suggested that the seizing of Indians lands was wrong, Winthrop replied that God had given the Pilgrims their title and banished the dissenter from the colony.

But other men of religion picked up the task of "spreading the Word" even to benighted natives. Successor church groups gave generous aid not only to the Indians but to other—colonial—peoples all over the world. In the nineteenth century, the American Board of Commissioners for Foreign Mission founded schools and hospitals over much of Africa and Asia. The Commissioners were not wholly altruistic: they hoped that what they did would cause the recipients to convert to their particular brand of Christianity.

Their activities were supplemented during the First World War by the privately-administered Near East Relief Society. Other non-governmental, sometimes secular, organizations followed and spread across Asia and Africa. Notable among them was the Rockefeller Foundation in China.

The aim of these groups, both religious and secular, was to share America's good fortune; inevitably, their activities created what amounted to love for America and gratitude toward Americans.

The effect on the American image abroad was dramatic: when President Woodrow Wilson set about his "crusade", he was greeted not as the head of a state but as a figure unknown in international affairs, a messiah. Europeans, Asians and Africans, who did not know of his unsavory record on domestic civil rights, virtually worshiped him.

Their admiration was not shared by Americans who agreed more with Wilson's attacks on civil liberties and his military invasions of America's neighbors than his ringing proclamations on human freedom and wellbeing in foreign affairs. He did not address his "Fourteen Points" speech to Americans, and, if they heard of them, they found them irrelevant. They withdrew into their domestic pursuits, first into the fun and frenzy of "Roaring Twenties" and then into the misery and anger of the Great Depression of the 1930s. American concern for the world bottomed out.

The Second World War changed all that. Americans realized that they could not withdraw from the world.

So, as the war ended, the American government did what no other victor had ever done: in the generous and far-sighted Marshall Plan they helped the defeated to rebuild. Of course, just as the missionaries had a second purpose in their aid, so had the government. The one aimed to make recipients into Christians and the other to make recipients into supporters of American political policy.

In the aftermath of the war, our mirror, like the one in the fairy tale of Snow White, shows us "who is the fairest of all." We see ourselves. We seek peace and wellbeing for all peoples; we help them with generous aid to uplift them from poverty; we rush to assuage their pains after wars and natural catastrophes, we "build" nations, topple tyrannies, spread democracy and uphold the rule of law.

If others do not see these virtues, they must be myopic, jealous or simply hateful. To us, it is disturbing that numbers of other peoples apparently do not see the image we see in our mirror. Increasingly, we are forced to recognize that numbers of other peoples do not see the image we see in our mirror. Worse, we are aware that their numbers are increasing.

As I have pointed out elsewhere, when as a young man I traveled throughout Latin America, Africa and Asia, I was everywhere warmly welcomed. Even in the "bad lands" of remote deserts and mountains, villagers and nomads would feed me even if they were hungry and if anyone tried to harm me it would have had to be over their dead bodies. Although alone and unarmed, I was everywhere an honored guest.

Today I would risk being shot—or perhaps have my head chopped off—in many of the same places. This is distressing for me personally and should be alarming for our nation. Ultimately, it may "blowback" against our national security. We need realistically to examine it rather than pretending that it is simply wrong or that it does not exist. So, what has happened?

To find out, look back at earlier times. We know that generous aid was given by Americans to peoples all over the world in the nineteenth century mainly because

Americans thought it was the right thing to do.

Today, aid is regarded as a tool in the attempt to control other people. Aid programs are sold to the American public by specifically proclaiming this aim. In practical terms, each administration, including the two I served, realized that they could not get Congressional funding unless the funds were justified as part of our military security program.

Altruism was deliberately cast aside. To talk of helping people either in the name of God or decency was a sure way to lose an appropriation. The surest way to get a program approved was to put it in the budget of the War Department.

Since the recipients understood our objectives—all they had to do was to read our newspapers to do so—they took the aid we gave but were less grateful for it than their fathers and grandfathers had been for private aid. Snow White's magic mirror showed on each of its two sides, a different face.

I ask you now to consider America's first experience in foreign colonialism, the Philippines side of the Spanish-American war of 1898.

At that time, the US army was composed of only 16,000 officers and men. But, as intended in the Constitution it was backed up by state militias which, as it turned out, did most of the fighting. The fighting in the Philippines was America's first foreign counterinsurgency.

Fortuitously, just before that war broke out, a British officer, Colonel (later General) C.E. Callwell published a guidebook on colonial warfare. Unlike the major European wars, he argued, colonial wars were small=scale, not fought by armies in fixed locations and so required new tactics. The tactics he advocated were actually not new; they had been practiced for years by Americans against the Indians and by Europeans in Africa and Asia. But, they had been partially forgotten. Callwell reminded us. In his very different way, he was as much a messiah as Woodrow Wilson. Those with guns followed him.

The wars that inspired him were terrible because they were "peoples' wars" and were virtually unwinnable by regular means. They could last forever. So they were (as Callwell wrote) "what regular armies have most to dread."   There were no front limes, no safe areas, no laws of war. Against guerrillas or insurgents, he wrote, colonial war must be extremely brutal: it must aim at destroying what the enemy most valued—the sanctity of his home, the safety and honor of his family and his means of earning a living. Only if the insurgent were completely cowed could the colonial rule become secure. So how did this play out in the Philippines?

As we looked into our side of Snow White's mirror, we saw that America was liberating the Philippines from the exploitive, brutal tyranny of the previous colonial power, Spain. It was against Spain that the Filipinos had been struggling for independence.

Altruistically, we just wanted to help them so we

disavowed any selfish interest. President William McKinley put it clearly: American policy was to help the people of the Philippines achieve independence. Lest he be misunderstood, he publicly proclaimed that "forcible annexation [like other imperialist nations were doing elsewhere would be] criminal aggression."

The Filipino insurgents—then seen as "Freedom Fighters" —were delighted and grateful. So, when the American fleet defeated the Spanish fleet in Manila Bay in 1898, the insurgents proclaimed a republic and welcomed the incoming American troops as "redeemers."

It was not long, however, before relations soured.

American officials on the spot regarded the Filipinos, as Rudyard Kipling memorably put it in explaining the "White Man's Burden," to be "Half-devil and half-child." Did the Filipinos deserve to be free? Could they even manage freedom? And, more concretely, who was entitled to the fruits of victory over the Spaniards?

Keeping the Philippines was of course tempting, but was it "right?"

No one was quite sure. So, President McKinley sought Divine guidance. As he wrote, he "went down on my knees and prayed Almighty God for light and guidance." His God was very accommodating. God replied, McKinley said, "...take them all."

So McKinley did. He dropped America's Filipino

would-be friends, the freedom fighters, and worked out a deal with Spain. He "bought" the Philippines and by extension the Filipinos themselves for 20 million dollars.

Peering through their side of the magic mirror, the provisional Philippine government was, of course, furious.

That was no surprise. The commander of the American troops warned that the majority of the people "will regard us with intense hatred…" He was right. In short, we began to view the former "Freedom Fighters" as "terrorists."

This is a transformation that would occur time after time in area after area over our lifetimes.

"Blowback" came when an American soldier killed a Filipino soldier. That was the beginning of the Philippine "insurrection." "Incident" followed terrorist attack and led to massacre. How to "pacify" the country was the urgent question.

Colonel Callwell had the answer. He recommended the use of "flying columns" [the ancestors of today's Special Forces] to strike at once on sign of trouble by and burning their dwellings."

The American soldiers, most of whom were Middle Western farm boys who had joined the National Guard for a little extra money or recreation, knew nothing of the far-off country. A contemporary humorist scoffed that the average American had not known "whether the Philippines were islands or canned goods…" The uncomfortable part-time soldiers just wanted to go home. So, when attacked by people they did not understand, they became fearful and angry. They quickly adopted Callwell's advice, burning villages and torturing captive Filipinos.

The American soldiers were the inventors of waterboarding—nearly drowning bound prisoners by forcing water down their throats. And they showed their hatred of the natives by referring to them in the already familiar word "niggers" and inventing a new word for them, "gubus."

On their side, not having modern weapons or military training, the Filipinos fell back on "the weapon of the weak," guerrilla warfare.

Callwell's battle plan had become a self-fulling prophecy.

By 1900 America had 150,000 soldiers in the Philippines. In the next two years, they suffered 6,000 casualties while killing tens of thousands of Filipinos. Fighting between the American army and the insurgents was as bitter as had been the wars of extermination against the Native Americans.

In our eyes, bringing law and order, reorganizing society, creating government and, hopefully uplifting the people, however much was destroyed in making such activities possible, were a necessary component of America's role in bettering the world.

In the eyes of many non-Americans, to the contrary, our actions were neither necessary nor welcome. Constantly repeated surveys of opinion show that the early Filipinos led what later was to become a parade of other peoples, many of whom have come to regard us as brutal, avaricious and destructive.

* * *

The contrast between the two sides of Snow White's magic mirror became evident already in the time of President Woodrow Wilson. I have mentioned that Europeans regarded him as a superhuman figure sent by God to deliver mankind from the scourge of war. But even before he entered the White House, Wilson had begun to call himself an imperialist. As David Foglesong has written, "No president has spoken more passionately and eloquently about the right of self-determination. Yet no president has intervened more often in foreign countries."

While promising to keep America out of the European war, Wilson sent American forces into Haiti and the Dominican Republic and twice into Mexico while telling the Mexicans that our invasions were in no sense an infringement of Mexican sovereignty. The postwar military intervention he ordered in Russia is today almost totally forgotten, at least by us. And he condoned what today we call "dirty tricks" to accomplish his objective. Just as we later tried to murder Castro, Nasser and other leaders, Wilson had the US government attempt to poison the Mexican President, Pancho Villa.

In domestic affairs also we have to admit that his record was not attractive. He instigated or at least tolerated attacks on the German-American community, on those who opposed (as he himself had done) America's entry into the European war, critics of his policy, the radical Left and recent immigrants.

Yet, at the same time as he was carrying out these policies, Wilson was proclaiming his "Fourteen Points," struggling against the European imperialists would divide the spoils of war amongst themselves and attempt to silence the voices of the emerging nations of Africa and Asia.

Many have charged that he—and by extension all of us, benevolent and right-thinking or at least right-talking Americans down to and including President Barak Obama—are hypocrites. While Wilson was the father of the League of Nations he did not prevent it from being turned into the "Polite" white man's way of carrying the "burdens" of the less-polite white man. Ineffective in Europe, the League of Nations was used to justify colonialism in Africa and Asia.

* * *

My reading of American history convinces me that we are a warring people. War, I think we can fairly say, has always been a fundamental feature of our national culture and we have from the beginning used it, time after time, to grow as a nation not only geographically but also socially and politically.

The First World War integrated the German part of our society—Schmidt became Smith. And the Second World War began the revolution that led our first black president to the White House. Attitudes toward war have played crucial roles in our evolution. They have energized our people, swept us across the Continent, given us a taste of empire, and enabled us to overcome powerful enemies. But, they have also led to great wrongs and even greater dangers.

Recognition of danger encouraged us to acquire the tools of war. I suggest that we might think of them as being like a pistol. Firing it is sometimes forced upon us, but, even kept in the holster it shapes our attitude and our actions., At worst, it can be used by ambitious leaders to shape or control our way of life. Brought into play, it can threaten or destroy our civic culture.

War is not a new challenge to our system nor is it uniquely American, but controlling it is, I believe, so urgent an issue today that we must understand all of its ramifications and effects as fully as possible.

Americans have never been willing to see the harsh reality of intervention and counterinsurgency. We were sure that we went into the Philippines with the very best of intentions—to bring democracy and modern habits to a backward people. In other wars, as in Vietnam, we proclaimed that we intervened legally at the request of a constituted government to protect it against foreign subversion or invasion. Where we did not have an invitation, as in Iraq, Afghanistan, Somalia and Libya, we invaded to destroy ugly tyrannies. We did these things, at least in part, because we had the pistol in our holster. And using it seemed to most of us—at least at the beginning of each intervention—moral, legal and beneficial. Some, perhaps even all of these regimes were tyrannies, but the aftermath of our interventions suggest that the medicine was worse than the disease. Nor, however powerful the medicine, was the "disease" often cured. War has come to seem more of a norm than an exception, more of an end than of an acceptable means and more of a patriotic duty than a policy to be judged.

So, in the last decades we have moved from one war to the next with virtually no pauses for consideration.

In my next talk, I will discuss how our Founding Fathers worried about the prospect of such actions and what they laid out at the Philadelphia Constitutional Convention in 1787 to create safeguards to protect us. Their deliberations are the subject of my next talk, but today leave you the frightening words of a great practitioner in the art of destroying societies and states in aggressive war. Hermann Göring, after he could no longer play a lead role in the game of nations, famously he told his jailers how rulers can use war:

"…of course the people don't want war," he said. "Why should some poor slob on a farm want to risk his life in a war when the best he can get out of it is to come back to his farm in one piece? Naturally the common people don't want war: neither in Russia, nor in England, nor for that matter in Germany. That is understood. But after all, it is the leaders of a country who determine the policy and it is always a simple matter to drag the people along, whether it is a democracy or fascist dictatorship, or a parliament or a communist dictatorship. Voice or no voice, the people can always be brought to the bidding of the leaders. That is easy.

"All you have to do is tell them they are being attacked, and denounce the peace makers for lack of patriotism and exposing the country to danger. It works the same in any country."

War and its necessary component, militarism, as Göring saw it, is the trump card in the game of power politics. He was not interested in the other side of Snow White's magic mirror. But the men who founded our country had a different view and took upon themselves a different task. How to protect our republic from the dangers of militarism and the terrible costs of war.

DEALING WITH MILITARISM

In my first talk, I discussed the role of colonialism and the fascination with war that Americans express in thought and action. I now turn back the clock to the Constitutional convention in 1787 to address how, from our earliest days as a nation, we have been excited by— and yet also frightened of—the ability of the military as an institution and of the military as a mindset to engage us in war.

I will go into detail on these issues because I believe that they are the most important touchstones we have to evaluate our current problems and potentials and because it appears that so few Americans know much about our social contract, the Constitution.

To judge the legality of our actions and to uphold the essential principles, jurists (of whom I am not one) today often act as historians (of whom I am one). Like historians, the lawyers and judges go back to the authors and events that shaped its construction.

This is not an arcane activity: the laws that affect our daily lives today are matched — or should be matched — against Constitutional standards. The Constitution sets out the only agreed benchmarks we have to determine how we can live together reasonably peacefully in one territory. Without it, we would be faced with anarchy.

Yet, as a prominent historian of America, Gordon Wood, has written, "Most universities have long since given up teaching undergraduate courses in American constitutional history, and most of those few remaining professors who do teach it are retiring and not being replaced."

A poll conducted a few years ago found that more than one in three Americans did not know in what century the American revolution happened and probably even fewer could have said when the Constitution was written or what it mandated.

So, I ask your indulgence. If I repeat what you already know, I would be delighted. And, if I supply any new information or insights, perhaps you may find my doing so to be useful.

I find it useful to think of the Constitution as a tree. Then we can ask why it was planted; in what "soil" its roots were set, how its trunk and branches took shape at the 1787 Constitutional Convention and how successive judges and political leaders have grafted new branches to it so that it shapes the America we have today. I take up first, the soil in which the Constitutional tree was planted.

* * *

What brought the men who gathered in Philadelphia in the uncomfortable state house during the hot and humid summer of 1787 was failure.

During the Revolutionary war, when it came to national interests, General George Washington found that even in the midst of battle, militia troops—that is, the people under arms—had a habit of running away, occasionally without even firing their weapons. Their commander, George Washington regarded them as nearly worthless cannon fodder.

In truth, despite our pride in the Spirit of '76, that Spirit is more evident in retrospect than it was in practice then. One witness, the chief engineer of the Continental Army, the French volunteer Louis Duportail, lamented, "There is a hundred times more enthusiasm in any Paris cafe [for the American revolution] than in all the colonies together."

Many American colonists kept focused on their private interests, sold food and equipment to the British Army and starved Washington and his troops at Valley Forge; others found it more profitable (and safer) to kill Indians for land than to fight the British for independence. This is not surprising: we see the same shortfalls of ardor for independence and national well-being today among the formerly colonial peoples of Africa and Asia.

Making the transition from colonialism to independence is usually a very slow process and during the time it takes to create a sort of national esprit de corps the transition experiences many set-backs.

We see these failures, disillusionments and bouts of lawlessness glaringly in shaky regimes and "failed states" in much of the world today. Often the newly liberated people come to feel nostalgia for the former regime. As they look around themselves, they see that former colonial auxiliaries have frequently become oppressive armies and the former freedom fighters often become corrupt tyrants or warlords.

Post- revolutionary America hovered on the brink of a similar anarchy. True, the Colonists had won the war of the Revolution but, in the peace that followed, America was what we would today call a failed state. The first attempt at forming the new country, the Confederation, had not worked. The "people" had seen that their sacrifices had not brought the millennium.

The mood of the American public, as reported throughout the former colonies, was one of confusion, dejection and anarchy. Everyone was distressed. Some even advocated returning to the British empire.

As the yellow press would later coin the phrase, "the public was "seething." The governing institution, the Confederation Congress, the successor to the Continental Congress, had not "taken." It could not cope with the strong-willed independence of the several states; it could not ensure "domestic tranquility," nor, any more than the British, could it prevent the restless colonists from provoking war with the Indian nations along the frontier. In short, Americans were suffering from what I have called in describing societies in Africa and Asia, post-colonial malaise.

The more established—that is the earlier—immigrants who had been running the colonies realized that they must bring a sense of order.

That was why they were gathering to plant a new "tree."

What about the "soil" into which they were thrusting their spades?

It would be almost unimaginable to young Americans today. In the context of 1787, and except for dress and language, the delegates would not have felt out of place in Calcutta, Lagos, Mogadishu or the capital of any African or Asian failed state today.

The streets of Philadelphia, then America's most "advanced" city, were open sewers, with swarms of mosquitoes and flies feeding on feces of animals and humans; crowds of immigrants from many lands jostled against one another and against the roaming pigs that were the only effective collectors of garbage; bathing was little practiced; even clean drinking water was a luxury beyond the reach of the indigent. Yellow fever repeatedly ravaged the population until, a decade later, wooden pipes were installed to provide reasonably clean drinking water.

The street people who milled about outside the relative elegance of the State House were strangers one to another. Their languages, cultures, dress and deportment did not evoke a sense of shared nationality.

What apparently they did share was drunkenness. Drunkenness led easily and quickly to violence and was anticipated at every hand. Gentlemen wore swords, sometimes hidden in canes, and often carried pistols. There was little civil authority: every man was on his own.

Recognizing the failings of their attempt to create stable governing institutions, the Confederation Congress had authorized the holding of a convention to amend the Articles of Confederation.

Amending the Articles of Confederation was the official mandate of the Philadelphia convention, but the delegates took their authority beyond what had been licensed. They planned not to amend but to replace the existing government.

Put baldly, what they were doing amounted to a *coup d'état.*

And for that reason, the delegates determined to hold their discussions in secrecy.

Not surprisingly, one of the first points on which they agreed was to sacrifice such little comfort as they could get from open windows by covering them in blinds and demanding that what took place in the hall of the state house not be revealed to outsiders. They realized they had to be careful to avoid what Delegate Pierce Butler of South Carolina called (with good reason) "licentious publications."

So the delegates sweltered together as they conspired.

Today, it has become fashionable to criticize them, but the delegates were an extraordinary group. Many had fought in the Revolutionary war—General George Washington was unanimously elected their president. Colonel Alexander Hamilton was one of the most influential delegates. As a group, the delegates shared generations of tradition and years of experience, even under British rule, in running the governments of their colonies. They were sure of themselves. As their conversations demonstrate, they were well-read and their linguistic ability—particularly in Greek and Latin—would have put to shame many of today's university faculties. They were nearly all members of the small Protestant, male, white elite. While they were determined to create a republic, they were not sentimental about the people. They did not expect the new citizens to be able "to establish justice, insure domestic Tranquility, provide for the common defence, promote the general Welfare, and secure the Blessing of Liberty." They hoped that public responsibility might come about in the future, but in the meantime, they believed that they had to act in the name of the people. What they aimed to do was to provide a legal structure, a matrix, into which the activities of the people could safely be placed.

They assumed that they, America's "most experienced & highest standing Citizens," as Delegate (and later President) James Madison described them, could create a matrix or framework in which their lofty aims had a chance of being achieved. That framework was the Constitution.

They were driven together by their shared perception that the Articles of Confederation had not worked. The confederation that had emerged during the Revolution was an attempt to hold the colonies together (to win the war against Britain) and to provide (after independence had been achieved) "domestic tranquility." It had barely, but just barely, sufficed for the first task but failed in the second. It was too weak. That it was weak—intentionally weak—was understandable, perhaps inevitable under the circumstances. After all, the Revolution had been undertaken to break loose from an authoritarian government — the British monarchy. And, at that time no one, certainly not they, knew how to balance authority with freedom.

They were not alone in worrying about the results of independence. Settlement after settlement, town after town, expressed its frustration and anger to state governments, and in various conventions delegations and individuals denounced the idea that sovereignty could be delegated to any official body. "People Power" was the sense of politics throughout the land.

Contemporary Americans were natural anarchists.

In the context of this mood, law and order was collapsing, and even while the Continental Congress was still in existence it could not protect either particular interests or the common interest.

Members of the elite were so disturbed by the current malaise that they delved into the history of the ancient

Roman republic and contemporary European states—particularly England—to see how other peoples had handled the definition and practice of government.

The less-widely-read general public was not so philosophical or abstract as the aristocracy but they too were fearful and were often angry.

The attitudes of both groups were largely predetermined by the political, economic and social system that had evolved over the previous century. The essential feature of that system was the division of the land into thirteen nearly self-governing colonies. Each had its own customs of government. From having been separate colonies, each had come to think of itself as a state. However, the Revolution had taught them that separately, they could not defend themselves.

Thus, by their experience in the war of the Revolution, they were concerned about the danger of foreign invasion. But by reading and reflecting, they were deeply worried about the cost of what would have been required to prevent attacks against themselves and their property. It was in the context of their aspirations and fears—the "soil"—in which they deliberated on planting the new tree.

How remarkable that deliberation was we can see by comparing what they were doing with what has been happening—or usually not happening—elsewhere in our own times. Over much of Asia and Africa, in the aftermath of decolonization, successor local elites continue to tear apart their emerging societies and the physical inheritance of the colonial period. The Founding Fathers, as land owners and community leaders were determined not to let this happen in America.

Being relatively isolated even from contact with one another—many had not met before they gathered in Philadelphia and contact among them was mainly by sporadic and expensive post or gossip-driven press—they were acutely aware of how small, poor, deeply-divided and weak was their new country.

Effectively, the "America" that was becoming a new nation- was just a narrow band along the coast between the Atlantic Ocean and the Allegheny mountains.

Widely separated settlements were mostly just towns or even villages. Moving among them was expensive and slow. Going from Boston to New York took three or four days while Philadelphia to Nashville took about three weeks. It was usually cheaper, less dangerous and far more comfortable to go from American to England by ship than to be jostled along inland trails. The mails were inadequate substitutes. Few had friends or relatives in other places, and as late as 1800 only one letter per person was posted each year. Literacy was weak and posting a letter in New York to Charleston, South Carolina cost the equivalent of a laborer's weekly wage.

These facts of life were not something they read about but rather were the experiences of everyday life. At least the men who wrote the Constitution realized how weak, scattered and backward their new country was. This realization led them to spend much of their thought on the danger of further war. Had they stopped there, we would not have had the Constitution they gave us.

But they also realized, from their readings, that it was not just the destruction, pillage and casualties of actual war that constituted the danger. Rather, it was the fear of these terrible costs that constituted the gravest threat to freedom and the ability to enjoy the good life which were their aims.

What we know of their deliberations—mainly the account written by James Madison—is filled with references to the woeful experiences of Greece, Rome and contemporary Europe in quest of "security." And their conversations bear witness to the deliberations of the great European (to them, recent) philosophers and legal commentators. Since we also know that they shared long evenings over well-lubricated, rich and heavy meals, we can imagine that their months together constituted a sort of running seminar on governance and on the propensity of government to become tyranny.

Put in terms of the analogy I drew of the document they were developing to a tree, what were the seedlings they were trying to plant?

The first answer is that they read widely and surprisingly deeply. They virtually memorized Montesquieu's The Spirit of the Laws and imbibed Sir William Blackstone's *Commentaries* on English common law which they assumed to be fundamental to their conception of government. Many also read Emmerich de Vattel's The Law of Nations, copies of which Benjamin Franklin had ordered and for years had circulated among men in public life because, as he said, "the circumstances of a rising state make it necessary frequently to consult *The Law of Nations.*"

The second answer is perhaps more compelling. The delegates had been through a remarkable series of personal experiences: first, the years of agitation leading up to the Revolution which were followed by the often-bitter struggle with the British rulers. During the Revolution, they learned about armies painfully and first hand because the partly mercenary British army had to live off the land and stole what it needed. It was often compelled to fight a guerrilla war. In this insurgency, civilians suffered.

But their suffering was uneven and inconstant. By modern standards, it was relatively mild, so, although it led to expulsion or flight of many Loyalists, it deeply divided those who remained. Finally, the Revolutionaries — and the many who had just stood aside—came to feel a gnawing sense that it may have been for naught.

All these experiences were compacted into very recent years. We must remember that in May 1787 when the delegates met at Philadelphia, independence was little more than three years old. The Treaty of Paris that ended the war with Great Britain was signed only in 1783; memories of the Revolution, the occupation and British rule were still fresh for some but almost painless for others. For many, wartime was a time of prosperity. In short, there was no single revolution but several different revolutionary experiences And, the lessons to be drawn were as diverse as were the experiences.

The single point on which delegates agreed was the quest for "domestic tranquility" was essential.

Thus, while some of the delegates, notably Alexander Hamilton, greatly admired the British monarchy as an institution, and wished to copy it hoping to achieve in America what it had seemed to have achieved in England, others saw the monarchy as painfully and proximately represented by the British army. It was armies that Hamilton's fellow delegates feared, The very idea of a standing army was anathema. Founding Father James Madison spoke for probably most Americans and certainly for those who wrote the Constitution when he said:

"A standing military force, with an overgrown Executive will not long be safe companions to liberty. The means of defense against foreign danger have been always the instruments of tyranny at home. Among the Romans it was a standing maxim to excite a war, whenever a revolt was apprehended. Throughout all Europe, the armies kept up under the pretext of defending, have enslaved the people."

How could a republic cope with this danger?

The great conservative, Alexander Hamilton argued that Americans should just give the president, who was the American version of the king, life-time tenure. Only if the chief executive felt safe in his august position, Hamilton thought, would he refrain from subverting the regime. That is, if he felt endangered, he would use his power "to prolong his powers [and] in case of war, he would avail himself of the emergency to evade or refuse a degradation from his place."

In short, war, perhaps stimulated by a would-be despot's fear, could destroy the Republic and render inoperative the system the Founding Fathers were striving to put in place.

The other delegates were not willing to go so far as Hamilton even to defend the republic. They thought it was both possible and wise just to trim the claws of any would-be despot. The claws were the armed forces so they must be kept small, on short rations and balanced by popular forces.

From Montesquieu's *Spirit of the Laws*, the writers of the Constitution concluded that they must keep the armed forces within strict bounds. Such few as they thought would be required to defend the land should not be a foreign or mercenary force. Such a force would owe the republic no loyalty. And even native troops should be under the command of the civilian government which "should have a right to disband them as soon as it pleased." Moreover, while serving under arms, "the soldiers should live in common with the rest of the people; and no separate camp, barracks, or fortress should be suffered..."

But, Montesquieu continued, unless they are carefully controlled, the public allows armies to aggregate power and stake out their own objectives: "It is natural for mankind to set a higher value upon courage than timidity, on activity than prudence, on strength than counsel..." The public will idolize soldiers and look down on their civilian leaders. Thus, he argued, the public will ever be tempted to accept their right to represent the nation, and they will seize the opportunity to convert a civil government into a military government, "This," he pointed out, "was the fate of Rome and could be the fate of all republics."

Thus, as James Madison later wrote in *Federalist* 41, "A wise nation...whilst it does not rashly preclude itself from any resource which may become essential to its safety, will exert all its prudence in diminishing both the necessity and danger of resorting to [the creation of a standing army] which may be inauspicious to its liberties."

Listening to the delegates, one hears that they wanted to seat political power in "the people." As Madison put it in *Federalist* 39, they believed that government "derives all its powers directly or indirectly from the great body of the people."

But, as men of experience in running their own affairs, they distrusted the people. They saw in the events then taking place all over the new country signs of ignorance, fickleness and propensity to violence.

So the Constitution they were devising had also the aim, although not explicatively stated, what Gouverneur Morris of New York and Pennsylvania did openly say, "to save the people from their most dangerous enemy, themselves." For Alexander Hamilton, the people was a 'great beast.'

Here is how the delegates perceived the issue of the power to make war. They felt they had to address head-on and make absolutely clear the issue of who or what agency of government could take this momentous step. In Madison's notes we can almost hear their voices. Let us listen for a few moments to their voices on Friday, August 21, 1787 as they wrote the Constitution:

* * *

"Mr. [Charles] Pinckney [of South Carolina] opposed the vesting of this power [to make war] in the Legislature. Its proceedings were too slow…

It would meet but once a year. The House of Representatives would be too numerous for such deliberations. The Senate [he thought] would be the best depositary, being more acquainted with foreign affairs and most capable of proper resolutions. If the States are equally represented in [the] Senate, so as to give no advantage to large States, the power will notwithstanding be safe, as the small have their all at stake in such cases as well as the large States.

"'It would be singular,'" he went on, "'for one authority [the House of Representatives] to make war, and another [the Senate] to make peace.'

"Mr. [Pierce] Butler [also of South Carolina] objected, saying, 'The objections against the Legislature lie in great degree [also] against the Senate.' He was for vesting the power in the President, who will have all the requisite qualities, and will not make war but when the Nation will support it.

"Mr. Pinckney also found this delegation of power to be a great danger. While he favored 'a vigorous Executive' [he] was afraid the Executive powers of the existing Congress might extend to peace & wars [which would enable] 'the Executive to become a monarchy, of the worst kind, to wit an elective one.'

"Mr. Madison and Mr. [Elsbridge] Gerry [of Massachusetts] moved to insert 'declare,' striking out [the words] 'make' war [from the text under discussion]; leaving to the Executive [only] the power to repel sudden attacks.

"Mr. [Roger] Sherman [of Connecticut] thought [the proposed wording] stood very well. The executive should be able to repel and not to commence war. 'Make' is better than 'declare' the latter narrowing the power too much.

"Mr. Gerry [objecting, said that he] 'never expected to hear in a republic a motion to empower the Executive alone to declare war.'

"Mr. [Oliver] Ellsworth [also of Connecticut, said] 'there is a material difference between the cases of making war and making peace. It should be more easy to get out of war, than [to get] into it. War also is a simple and overt declaration, peace [is] attended with intricate & secret negotiations.'

"Mr. [George] Mason [of Virginia] was against giving the power of war to the Executive, because [he was] not safely to be trusted with it; or to the Senate, because not so constructed to be entitled to it. He was for clogging rather than facilitating war; but [he was] for facilitating peace. He preferred 'declare' to 'make.'

"On the motion to insert [the word] declare — in place of make, it was agreed to."

That is how the text of the Constitution emerged — In Article One, Section Eight, Paragraphs 1 and 11 the Constitution states that "The Congress shall have the Power…to declare war."

After the Convention, writing in *Federalist* 4, John Jay [of New York who was the first Chief Justice of the Supreme Court] caught what was probably a general attitude of the public and certainly was that of the Founding fathers, when he warned that "monarchs will often make war when their nations are to get nothing by it."

Beware, he went on, they will do this "for purposes and objects merely personal, such as, a thirst for military glory, revenge for personal affronts; ambition, or private compacts to aggrandize or support their particular families, or partisans."

It was not long before Jay's list could have been expanded to the desire of candidates to win elections by appearing to the defenders of national honor or protectors of national interests. War, or the threat of war, as several of our later presidents knew, can be ridden like the surf toward electoral victory.

In later writings, James Madison focused more generally on the division of powers in war making.

He argued that "Those who are to conduct a war cannot in the nature of things, be proper or safe judges, whether a war ought to be commenced, continued, or concluded. They are barred from the latter functions by a great principle in free government, analogous to that which separates the sword from the purse, or the power of executing from the power of enacting laws."

So what the Founding Fathers did was to limit the military in all the ways they thought would work. They planned to balance their little army— at that time the American army numbered only 718 men — with armed civilians in state militias that could be "Federalized" only "to execute the Laws of the Union, suppress Insurrections and repel Invasions..." They set this out in Article One, Section Eight, paragraph 15.

But they did not think this control system was sufficient and certainly not fool-proof.

So, they strengthened it. In Article One, Section Eight, paragraph 12, they specified that while Congress could "raise and support Armies...no Appropriation of Money shall be for a longer Term than two Years") and they had the Constitution rule that the Congress, not the president, was "To make Rules for the Government and Regulation of the land and naval Forces..." (Article One, Section Eight, paragraph 14).

In addition, despite the argument put forward by Alexander Hamilton for a lifetime tenure for the president, they limited his term to an electoral cycle of four years and restricted his power over the armed forces to carrying out the orders of the Congress. In Article Two, Section Two, paragraph 1, although he was designated as commander-in-chief, the president was to be what today we would call a chief operating officer rather than a chief executive officer. He could order the army or militia into action only when the Congress declared war (Article One, Section Eight, paragraph 11) or to repel invasion or to suppress insurrection (Article One, Section Eight, paragraph 15).

George Washington, who had been president of the Constitutional Convention and had become president of the new republic, affirmed this interpretation of the law in 1793 when he proclaimed that "The constitution vests the power of declaring war in Congress; therefore no offensive expedition of importance can be undertaken until after they [the members of Congress] shall have deliberated upon the subject and authorized such a measure."

*   *   *

I turn now to what has happened to the Constitutional "tree" since it first took root.

Although the issue of war was perhaps the most clearly stated and detailed of the injunctions spelled out in the Constitution, the delegates were aware that disagreements might come about. So, they ordered in Article Three, Section One and Section Two, paragraph 1 the creation of a Supreme Court.

In its first major rulings, 14 years after the Philadelphia Convention, the Court affirmed a straightforward reading of what the delegates had written, "The whole powers of war, being by the Constitution of the United States, vested in congress...the congress alone may declare war."

This reading of the Constitution was unchallenged during most of the following century. But an extraneous element had been introduced in 1800 into the issue of war powers that would come to haunt America in our times.

In a speech made in 1800 before the Congress the then-Congressman John Marshall coined a phrase to describe the military or foreign affairs power of the presidency. The phrase was "sole organ."

What Congressman Marshall argued was that the president, as the Constitution clearly states, "shall take care that Laws be faithfully executed." The presidency was, he suggested, the sole organ of government to implement the laws. As they related to war, the Laws began as motions that were passed by the Congress. Marshall did not suggest that in any way the presidency replaced the congress in creating law but only in carrying it out. He wrote that "The whole powers of war, being by the Constitution of the United States, vested in congress...the congress alone may declare war."

That was and remained the orthodox interpretation.

Almost half a century later, in 1848, the then Congressman Abraham Lincoln explained the reason for this division of powers when he wrote that,

"The provision of the Constitution giving the war-making power to Congress was dictated, as I understand it, by the following reasons. Kings had always been involving and impoverishing their people in wars, pretending generally, if not always, that the good of the people was the object. This, our Constitutional Convention understood to be the most oppressive of all Kingly oppressions; and they resolved to so frame the Constitution that no one man should hold the power of bringing this oppression upon us."

During the Civil War, the roles of the president and the Congress were again tested when ships were seized and had to be judged in what became known as the Prize Cases. In ruling on them, the Supreme Court again affirmed that "By the Constitution, Congress alone has the power to declare a national or foreign war [and the President] has no power to initiate or declare a war either against a foreign nation or a domestic State."

In summary, we have seen that up to roughly three generations after the writing of the Constitution, no question arose on the division of powers between the Congress (to declare war) and the Presidency (to execute the law as passed by the Congress). Indeed, it was to be another seventy years before this doctrine was challenged.

Challenged it has been in our lifetime. A legal basis has been brought forward to shift the balance of power between the President and the Congress and by extension to justify America's repeated engagement in war. Because this has been such an important, if little known or understood, transformation of America's role in international affairs and has "blown back" with such damaging effects on our sense of security, trust in one another and way of life, I will examine how it came about and why it is a violation of the word and spirit of the Constitution.

* * *

Here I must deal with the way later jurists have grafted onto the original "tree" of the Constitution new branches, creating what our great old philosopher Benjamin Franklin warned against, an "imperial presidency."

The issue has been defined by the phrase we have already met, "sole organ."

Simply stated, the question is, "Is the president both the sole author and the sole actor in actions particularly concerned with foreign affairs and the making of war?"

As I have said, the phrase, sole organ, was used in a speech by John Marshall when he was a Congressman, not when he later became a member of the Supreme Court. It was taken out of context, leaving aside the qualifying understanding that Marshall implied that the President was the "sole organ" in effecting a law that had been passed by the Legislature.

In an early test of the provision, President John Adams has been criticized for an unpopular decision—delivering to Great Britain a convicted criminal as required by a provision in a treaty with Great Britain.

Article Six, paragraph 2, of the Constitution specified that a treaty is "the supreme Law of the Land so rather than acting on his own, Adams appeared to be carrying out a Congressional order.

Or, did his action imply more wide-ranging and independent power? The question never was raised for nearly a century and a half.

The issue came finally before the Supreme Court in 1936. The key role in answering this question was played by Justice George Sutherland.

George Sutherland was an English immigrant who made it his life-long mission to argue "that the president must be given a free, as well as a strong hand." His attitude was manifested during the First World War when, like many other Americans including President Wilson, he was caught up in "war fever" of lynch mobs and massive incarceration.

That was Sutherland's political background; his legal application of his attitude came into focus in his reading of the Constitution and was set out in a case known as *The United States vs. Curtiss-Wright Export Corp.*

Briefly put, the case arose because in 1932 Curtiss-Wright was selling machineguns to Bolivia which was then engaged in a war with Paraguay. The two states were acting as proxies for Shell and Standard Oil, both of which believed that a province on the Bolivian-Paraguayan frontier had deposits of oil.

Attempting to keep the peace, the US government decided to stop the flow of arms. Thus, President Roosevelt "acting," as he proclaimed, "under and by virtue of the authority conferred in me by the said joint resolution of Congress," declared an embargo on the sale. Curtiss-Wright then violated the embargo and continued to sell arms. In response, the US sued.

The case gave the Supreme Court a chance to rule on the extent of presidential and congressional powers.

Justice Sutherland wrote for the Court, and his opinion,

quoted in turn in later decisions, provided the basis for the assertion of presidential power in our time for the "war on terror."

In essence, Sutherland argued that in time of war, American traditional rights and liberties lapsed. Further, he believed civil rights existed only in domestic law.

While there is no reason to believe that he would have approved of torture, the decision he wrote for the Supreme Court has been used to justify it and other practices. It has also been used to give the president license to invade other countries. So, it has been one of the most important decisions ever made by the Supreme Court.

Essentially what Justice Sutherland argued was that presidential power was far greater than had ever before been claimed, that "in international relations, the President is the "sole organ" of the Federal Government and that "unbroken legislative practice from the inception almost of the national government...must [despite the Constitution] often accord to him [the President] a degree of discretion and freedom which would not be admissible were domestic affairs alone involved and that the restrictive provisions of the Constitution were operative only in domestic affairs and of limited scope even then."

As a historian I find fundamental and indeed disqualifying faults in Sutherland's opinion and, consequently, in the use made of it to justify some of the worst abuses of our time. They deserve, indeed, demand our attention.

The first fault is Sutherland's assertions that "a steady stream [of presidential actions taken at his sole discretion] for a century and a half of time, goes a long way in the direction of providing the presence of unassailable ground for the constitutionality of the practice [of the President handling all aspects of foreign affairs]."

But, the acts he cites were authorized by Congress. Beginning with Jefferson and running through Lincoln this was true.

The only major exception was Andrew Jackson's disregard of the attempt by the Supreme Court to stop what Associate Justice John Story called "the iniquity of oppressing the [Cherokee] Indians and disregarding their rights."

I do not believe that any serious legal scholar today would argue that Jackson was acting constitutionally.

In the case on which he based his argument, Curtis-Wright, Roosevelt did not assert the powers Sutherland assigned to the presidency. As I have pointed out, he justified his action by citing the authority granted by the Congress: Congress was to decide policy and the Executive was to implement it. Not more and not less. On this point, Sutherland was wrong.

The second fault is that Sutherland based his argument for presidential overlordship on the assertion that the "States severally never possessed international powers… [And that, when the Revolution was ended in the 1783 peace treaty] the powers of extended sovereignty passed from the Crown not to the Colonies severally, but to the Colonies in their collective and corporate capacity as the United States of America…since the states severally never possessed international powers, such powers could not have been carved from the mass of state powers, but obviously were transmitted from…the Crown."

This is simply not true. The 1783 Treaty of Paris that ended the war specified that it was made between Great Britain on the one hand and on the other hand individually by each of the named thirteen "free, sovereign and independent states."

Indeed, at the time when sovereignty was passed to the states, they had no single chief executive and no single legislature. While the Continental Congress was mentioned in the Treaty, its sole function was to "earnestly recommend" to the states to restore properties that had been confiscated from British subjects.

Sutherland was simply wrong.

Third, while Sutherland thought of sovereignty as a single attribute, in America in those years it was diffuse. As is common in insurgencies, what amounted to "sovereignty" was dispersed. In the year before the best-known (Philadelphia) Declaration of Independence, nearly a hundred declarations of independence were proclaimed by self-governing local groups. As I have elsewhere written, one of these, in the frontier area of North Carolina, was the work of my great, great, great grandfather, General Thomas Polk.

Finally, fourth, Sutherland's assertion that the colonies had no international or foreign affairs role is also historically fallacious. What, after all, was the Revolution but an assertion of authority vis-à-vis what their governments had come to regard as a foreign power?

Each colony had set itself up as an independent entity to deal with the British. North Carolina established a Provincial Congress in 1774, and Massachusetts quickly followed. The Massachusetts declaration of self-government came from an armed revolt centered on Worcester that dissolved the 1691 Charter and took control of all the settled areas of the colony outside of British-occupied Boston. The Second Provincial Congress of New York during June 1775 refused permission for provisioning Royal Navy ships in its harbor, an act of treason as the British saw it or declaration of independence as the New Yorkers saw it.   The June 12, 1776 Virginia Declaration of Rights called for "the proper, natural, and self-defense of a free state" to be upheld by its own armed force. Other colonies followed. There is no sign that the colonies gave up their separate sovereignty. That they did not was, of course, the major reason for the 1787 Constitutional Convention.

And, during the Revolutionary War battles, the states separately—to George Washington's dismay—employed their own military forces under their own command. Throughout the Revolution, while the Continental Congress enrolled an army of its own, the "Continental Line," the states continued to maintain their separate militias.

Surely, each of the colonies or, as they proclaimed themselves to be, states, was engaged in foreign affairs. Foreign affairs—the struggle against Great Britain—was the essence of politics in each state. Indeed, it was the implication of their choice of the word "state" to replace the word "colony." A major attribute of statehood is, of course, the conduct of relations with other states.

As the American historian Gordon W. Wood has written, "When on July 4, 1776, Americans declared independence from the monarchy of Great Britain, they were faced with the formidable task of creating new republican governments. Their immediate focus was not on any central authority but on their individual state governments."

Sutherland's ignorance of history has had profound effects on our lives. His misreadings were cited to overturn the careful balancing of powers the Founding Father spelled out in Constitution. For this we have already paid a heavy price.

In short, Sutherland returned to the position the Founding Fathers rejected. He picked up the conclusion if not the justification of the proposal set out by Alexander Hamilton. He wanted America to have an elected king with virtually overwhelming power. Indeed, Sutherland went even further than Hamilton: his "king" was to have such power not only in foreign affairs but also in domestic affairs.

The more recent presidents have felt themselves justified in assuming ever increasing powers as Sutherland argued. They have done this, I believe both because of the natural inclination of rulers to aggrandize their positions and because they have tended to see international relations as taking place in what Thomas Hobbes had called a "state of nature." That is they considered relationships among states to take place in, a lawless world of actual or potential war of everyone against everyone.

And, from at least the dawning of the missile age, military and "security" experts have convinced civil leaders that they had to be able to engage in "rapid response." Waiting for Congressional sanction, which is necessarily slow. By appearing weak would encourage aggression. Consequently, many advocates of military action have fastened upon Sutherland's opinion to justify an America that would be swift— that is without Congressional sanction—in using "the sword."

What was—and remains today—the final step in Sutherland's impact on the nature of American governance is that the group the Founding Fathers thought they could rely upon to restrain the drift into despotism, the elected legislature, has abandoned its assigned role. It has generally given the chief operating officer its approval to be the chief executive officer of the American government.

As the eminent scholar of American Constitutional Law, Louis Fisher, has pointed out, this doctrine was cited in 1950 to justify President Truman's sending of troops to Korea, in 1966 to justify President Johnson's intervention in Vietnam and in 1994 to justify President Clinton's terrorism legislation.

More recently, it formed the basis for the memorandum written by John C. Yoo, then deputy assistant attorney general of the Office of Legal Counsel, which specifically justified the notion that the president was the "sole organ of the nation in its foreign relations, to use military force abroad."

Based as Yoo's argument was on a decision by the Supreme Court which, although as I have argued was fatally flawed, was still standing, President George W. Bush asserted his authority to invade Afghanistan and Iraq as Essentially, the memorandum certified President Bush's legal authority to invade other countries.

*   *   *

In the attempt to rein in the abuse of the Constitutional guards against excessive presidential powers and specifically the danger of "imperial" presidents plunging the country into war, came the War Powers Resolution, (PL 93-148, 87 Stat.555). President Nixon regarded it, rightly, as an attack on his powers. Passed over his veto on November 7, 1973, it aimed to "insure that the collective judgment of both the Congress and the President will apply to the introduction of United States Armed Forces into hostilities," and that "the President's powers as Commander in Chief are exercised only pursuant to a declaration of war, specific statutory authorization from

Congress, or a national emergency created by an attack upon the United States."

Twenty-eight years later, in the panicked wake of the terrorist attacks on the World Trade Center and the Pentagon, Congress passed Public Law 107-40 which effectively gave President Bush precisely those powers the writers of the Constitution sought to deny him. That is, to "use all necessary and appropriate force against those nations, organizations, or persons he determines [emphasis added] planned, authorized, committed, or aided the terrorist attacks that occurred on September 11, 2001, or harbored such organizations or persons, in order to prevent any future acts of international terrorism against the United States by such nations, organizations or persons."

Then, in October of the following year, the Congress passed Public Law 107-243 authorizing the President to use force to invade Iraq and did not require that Iraq be found to be guilty of the attacks on the United States. The president was not required to determine anything. He was set free to act as he desired.

Two aspects of the American action are thus highlighted in the Congressional resolutions: the first was that American forces were to be brought to bear not only on states but on individuals and nongovernmental groups and, second, resolutions 1511 and 1546 projected the creation of an "incoming Interim Government of Iraq." That is, they projected "regime change" in foreign lands as an aspect of American policy.

These shifts from the American Constitution's approach to presidential powers and to the issue of war have had profound effects on our lives today and will, I believe, continue far into the future.

But, to go full circle, I must return to the issue of war and peace as posed by the delegates at Philadelphia. Their decision was that the ultimate safeguard against unnecessary war was the Congress. It alone could declare war. They could not have imagined the transformation of that body as the society's desire about ability to pay for goods and services grew.

What happened was a series of more or less unrelated actions. The first was a decision, made roughly at the same time as the Supreme Court ruled on Presidential power, that authorized the sale of the airwaves for broadcasting. An attempt in the establishment of the Federal Communications Commission (the FCC) was made to ensure their use for public purposes, but the essential result was that the airwaves became commodities that could be sold by the minute to anyone with the money to buy them.

Purchase was very attractive for businesses but also for politicians. Whereas the American tradition put candidates literally on stumps to harangue small groups, first radio and then television gave them potentially vast audiences. But that access came at a large and enormously increasing cost.

To get the money to buy radio or television access

to the public became the essential task of a typical congressman. Members of the House of Representatives spent an average of nearly one and a half million dollars every two years to be reelected.

A sitting Congressman could, of course, ask for contributions from his constituents, but money came in drips and drabs. Successful politicians learned that the quickest, easiest and surest way to get the money to win elections was hiring themselves out to special interests.

Will Rogers put it bluntly, but perhaps with a smile on his face, "A fool and his money is soon elected."

Joking or not, Will Rogers was right. In 2016 an average of 95% of the winners in both the House of Representatives were those who spent the most. Prominent among the donors were war-related industries.

So public interest groups and commentators have for years sought ways to rein in the corruption of the system by the quest for money. Their efforts to return to something like the drafters of the Constitution had in mind have, at least so far, been defeated by the failure of the legislators to rule themselves.

The classically-minded Founding Fathers would not have been surprised. What the Congress was demonstrating was the modern version of the dilemma set out in Roman times, "who rules the rulers?" Patrick Henry gave a pessimistic answer when he wrote, "Show me that age and country where the rights and liberties of the people were placed on the sole chance of their rulers being good men, without a consequent loss of liberty."

A study of the members of the House of Representatives perhaps would not have shocked Henry, but it should shock us: At least 117 of the 535 members have been bankrupted at least twice; 7 have been charged with fraud; 8 have been arrested for shop lifting; and others have been charged with spousal abuse, writing bad checks and using or selling drugs. The personal reputations of a number of others are so questionable that they cannot obtain credit cards. And, when the charges are sufficiently public or damaging, the members are protected by a secret Congressional committee which can dispense public funds to settle law suits against them.

Indeed, it is hard to escape the application to the Congress of Isaiah 36:6 that the Founding Fathers put their trust in a pillar of government, the House of Representatives, that has turned out to be a broken reed on which if a man—and by extension a nation—leans, "it will enter his hand and pierce it."

Calls for reform and the curtailment of the selling of the services of the Congressmen received a major setback in rulings by the Supreme Court. In 2010 in the *Citizens United vs. Federal Elections Commission* case and in 2013 in the *McCutheson vs. Federal Election Commission* case the Court held essentially that there are no limits on contributions to Congressmen since corporations are (legally) "people" and lobbying is a form of "speech" which is protected for (real) people by the First Amendment to the Constitution that prohibits curtailment of free speech.

Clearly, we are in the midst of a great but nearly silent and unseen crisis similar to the one faced by our Founding Fathers in 1787.

So, in my final talk I will bring together the experiences that set patterns of action and the legal decisions that formed the American system of government and relate them to the challengers America has faced in world affairs and discuss how in our times they have impacted upon our lives and what has been the reaction of others to them.

A Warring People

In my previous two talks, I discussed the impact of colonialism and militarism on American society and what the Founding Fathers did to try to make American liberty more secure. I also discussed the changes their successors made. Now in this final session, I turn to what has been tried to enhance the chances of our achieving what I call Affordable World Security and what has diminished the chance of our doing so.

You don't need me to recount the flow of violence in the world—it pours over us every day in the media. Bombings, assassinations, renditions, torture, war and the resulting sense of insecurity have become the saga that describes our lives.

Instead, what I will do today is discuss and probe how the world in which we now live evolved at the end of the Second World War, how our government and its advisers tried to understand and cope with what they perceived as the threats to our security and how the Cold war and other challenges have affected our lives.

These are large and diffuse topics, and in the short time we have together I will be able to deal with only a few aspects of them and even on those I will have to skip much. I will try to be brief, but I will probably fail. So, I ask your indulgence.

I begin with two views, widely separated in time, on where we are today.

*   *   *

Speaking at the University of Chicago in 1950, the grand strategist of the Cold War, George Kennan, said that "The central puzzle" that confronted Americans then was the decline of American security. "A half-century ago," he continued, "people in this country had a sense of security vis-à-vis their world environment such as I suppose no people had ever had since the days of the Roman Empire. Today that pattern is almost reversed...We have before us a situation which, I am frank to admit, seems to me dangerous and problematical in the extreme... How did a country so secure become a country so insecure?"

That was 68 years ago. What has happened since? Have our policies, our efforts, our vast expenditure of talent and money resulted in the security we tried to achieve?

One answer was given last September by the official who is responsible for our major foreign affairs area, the chief of NATO. "The world," he said, "is at its most dangerous point in a generation." You will also have seen that the *Bulletin of The Atomic Scientists* has just moved us half a minute closer to "Midnight."

In fact, our country has been secure—at least in the sense that we were not engaged in hostilities somewhere only about 20 years since the 1787 Constitutional Convention. And, since the Vietnam war, we have engaged in almost non-stop conflicts throughout most of the world. What the editors of the *New York Times* called "America's Forever Wars" now have us engaged in military operations in at least 172 countries and territories. In them, more than a quarter of a million American servicemen and women, backed up nearly that many mercenaries and special agents have been carrying out the whole gambit of overt military and covert espionage activities.

In my book, *Crusade and Jihad,* I dealt with some of the reasons behind the dangers we face. I focused there on overseas events and particularly on the "blowback" of peoples throughout the world against imperialism, colonialism and foreign intervention.

Today, I will deal primarily with what America has done in its attempt to create security for itself. I will avoid, as much as possible, assessing blame, or giving credit but rather will analyze actions in terms of their success or failure.

To put our actions in perspective, I begin with what other nations have done that set the context in which we have operated and, indeed, established the very definition of security.

* * *

Is there really anything we can think of as security? That is, within the general aims of our society, is security possible? Dwight Eisenhower doubted it. "If you want total security" he said, "go to prison. There you're fed, clothed, given medical care and so on. The only thing lacking... is freedom."

I believe you will agree with me that that degree of security is not affordable. Indeed, trying to achieve it has costs that often make the medicine worse than the disease.

But security has been the prime objective of societies from the earliest times. Everywhere people built defensive barriers. First, the barriers were probably just piles of brush; later, the settled villagers began to build walls. Building them were Herculean tasks and destroying them became the immediate aims of their foes.

Already, in the little town of Jericho about 7000 BC—as we learned in the beautiful Afro-American spiritual—the "walls come a-tumbling down." In fact, the walls hardly needed to be destroyed to wreck the town; just the task of building them virtually destroyed it. It has been calculated that every inhabitant must have spent about a quarter of his adult life laboring by hand to quarry, carry and place as much rock and earth as would fill a large truck trailer. Workers hardly had time to herd animals or raise crops. Even at that huge expenditure of human muscle, walls didn't save Jericho; rather it sapped the town of its energy, its resources and ultimately its life.

We know that the inhabitants were killed, carried off or ran away and were replaced by invaders time after time so that their successors had to build or rebuild Jericho's walls at least 20 times.

But, almost everywhere and at all times, walls continued to be built. The Egyptian hieroglyph for "town" also meant "wall," and the Chinese ideograph for city, *ch'eng*, rises from the character for wall. The Great Wall of China, the *Ai,* and its smaller cousin, Hadrian's wall in England were the work of generations. Medieval Europe was divided into hundreds of walled towns. The cost of building and manning its defenses literally bled one of them, the beautiful little city of Sienna, to death.

We are at it again in our times—the Maginot Line, the Italian barrier along the Libyan-Egyptian and the French barrier along the Algerian-Tunisian frontiers, the Berlin Wall, the Israeli wall against the Palestinians—and today the Trump administration is trying to copy them along the Mexican frontier.

Common to all these efforts is that they are ruinously expensive and that they have never worked. So, the stronger, larger and better organized societies often set out to destroy their enemies in their own homelands. That was the origin and purpose of aggressive war.

From the time of the ancient Assyrians, the powerful carried war to their weaker neighbors much as Americans did to the Red Indians, the Boers did to the Bantu and the Chinese did to the Central Asian Zunghars. But no amount of military action brought more than temporary security.

Moreover, the creation and use of armies, like wall building, came with ruinous costs. Whole societies were transformed, corrupted or ruined by militarization. In medieval Italy, where warfare was endemic, a single campaign might cost a city-state ten times its annual revenue.

So it was that we owe to Florence two of the actions of governments that control so much of our lives today. Florence created the first European tax, the *catasto*, and when taxes did not suffice it also created the first system of public debt, the *monte commune*, the "mountain of debt." Today, we have enormously amplified both—we have had to do so because our wars cannot be paid for by taxation, and we will leave the bill to our grandchildren or even to their grandchildren. The mountain looms before us.

Even more detrimental than monetary cost, war is the militarization of society. As I have pointed out in my previous talk, our Founding Fathers knew that the pursuit of security through militarization transforms, subverts or curtails essential liberties and so weakens the civic institutions and practices it was supposed to protect. Indeed, as Henry L. Stimson, our great Secretary of War in whose name we meet today, presciently wrote back in 1932, unless some move is made to prevent war, "modern civilization might be doomed."

Stimson's answer to this danger was a peace convention, the Briand-Kellogg Pact for the Renunciation of War. It was signed by most independent states, but it too did not work. It was not long before Germany and Italy bombed and destroyed Republican Spain, Italy conquered Ethiopia and Japan pillaged and raped much of China.

The Axis Powers brought the evils of war to virtually the whole world, including our nation.

But hope springs eternal. Treaties are still being tried. Biological weapons were legally banned nearly half a century ago and chemical weapons were banned a few years later. However, despite the treaties, these horrible weapons continued to be manufactured, stored and occasionally used. Then, in July last year, 122 countries signed a treaty calling for the prohibition of nuclear weapons. But, of course, those that have the weapons did not sign. Their abstention did not "make war," but it accentuated the "apprehension of danger" that shapes our lives today.

Apprehension of danger of course, often leads to war, but even when it does not it weakens the most precious and most fragile of our cultural attributes, our sense of civilized life. This loss of the humane aspects of civilization is evident in the use of torture and other barbaric activities that not only impact upon the victims but also pervert those who employ them.

So, a few men tried to dig deeper into the question of why we all—not just the Americans but all members of our species—are warring peoples.

In his open letter of July 30, 1932 which is often referred to as the essay "Why War," Albert Einstein asked, "Is there any way of delivering mankind from the menace of war [which] has come to mean a matter of life and death for Civilization as we knew it. Despite all the zeal displayed, every attempt at solution has ended in a lamentable breakdown." This must be, he concluded, "Because man has within him a lust for hatred and destruction."

What can be done about this, apparently fundamental, human trait? Einstein decided that the best person to address this question was Sigmund Freud.

Freud offered Einstein neither solution nor solace. He believed that human nature is incorrigible. He thought that the only hope is to wrap mankind in what he called "a supreme court of judicature…with adequate executive force [because] any effort to replace brute force by the force of an ideal is, under present conditions, doomed to fail…there is no likelihood of our being able to suppress humanity's aggressive tendencies."

So what is the record of humanity's aggressive tendencies in our times?

Forgive me for indulging in the habits of a historian. I think we must dig into the past to understand the present. Merely reacting to or just regurgitating the litany of current events is of little benefit. We are daily regaled with them. I admit that I am also reacting against the attitude I encountered in government—'never ask what caused a given problem; let us just deal with what we see now.' Or, as the saying goes, "ready, shoot, aim."

I think it is important in trying to see what prevents us from feeling secure to know how America got involved with what we are now doing or trying to do.

*   *   *

There is no agreed place to begin discussion of the tumult of the last century, but it seems to me that the character and dimensions of the challenge we face today are marked by the strategic doctrines and tactical actions we can summarize, in more than jest, under the totem animals, the Lion, the Bear and the Eagle.

The British Lion had grabbed large chunks of the Mughal Empire in the eighteenth and nineteenth centuries and was feeding itself—and financing what we call the Industrial Revolution—from the rich Indian subcontinent. Having lost the American empire, King George III feared that without its Indian empire England would be "a toothless little beast, living off scraps." But with India under its control, Britain became a Lord of the World. So, the Lion roared and flailed away to acquire not only India but also its neighborhood and to keep everyone else out.

The most important "everyone else" was the Russian Bear. Starting with Ivan the Terrible, Russian tsars plunged down the Don and the Volga. They too wanted a piece of India. Peter the Great got as far as the Caspian Sea and when that route proved difficult his successors threw their armies into the Ottoman empire, attempting to break into the warm Mediterranean to sail toward India.

The epic and romanticized battles of the Lion and the

Bear—the Great Game in the towering mountains of Afghanistan and the Charge of the Light Brigade in the Crimea—were the nursery rhymes of generations of English statesmen including Winston Churchill.

All his life, Churchill was obsessed with blocking the Russian route to Britain's Indian empire. To him, that meant enabling the Ottoman empire to hold the "choke point" of the Turkish Straits. With a "cork" in place at Istanbul, the Russians would be bottled up in the Black Sea.

British strategy worked, but the Turks eventually played their part too well. In the First World War, when Britain and Russia had become allies, the Turks closed the Straits to both the Russians and the British and starved Russia into the 1917 Revolution.

War and revolution swept away the nineteenth century. In just a few years, both the Ottoman Empire and the Russian Empire collapsed and British India began the political evolution that would lead a quarter of a century later to its end.

The World changed but Churchill did not. Ever the imperialist, he kept to his strategy. If India would no longer be Britain's empire—though Churchill tried his best to prevent the coming of Indian independence —its "neighborhood" became a vital British interest. India's contribution to the empire was taken up by the oil fields of the Middle East. Without Middle Eastern oil, got cheap on the concessionary terms imposed by imperialism, Churchill feared that England would starve or become, as King George had feared long before, just a toothless little beast.

So, his overriding goal was to find a new chokepoint to confine the Russian bear—that bear, having grown a new coat, had become the Soviet Union. Since Turkey was no longer available, Churchill decided, the best barrier was Greece. He determined that Greece would become Britain's notional wall.

Churchill's strategy was actually not new; it was a holdover from the nineteenth century. Then the powerful countries treated the weaker countries like lifeless pieces to be arranged and moved around by the Great Powers. Churchill and many others followed the South African leader General Jan Smuts in thinking of the "Little Countries" as dominos.

Neither in Greece nor elsewhere did Churchill see that, in struggling for freedom, initially against the Nazis and the Fascists, societies had recast themselves as nations with their own aspirations. To him, Greece was still just a domino. He had little interest in and virtually no knowledge of what was happening in Greece.

What was happening was that the 1940 Axis invasion had driven out the Greek king, his army and his court. They ended up in Egypt under British control. But the king left behind the bureaucracy and the security forces of the former dictator, Iohannis Metaxas, who before the German invasion had been the effective ruler of Greece. In the 1930s, Metaxas had tried to turn Greece into a

Nazi state complete with Greek versions of the Gestapo, the SS and even the Hitler Youth. Metaxas had died, but the regime he established lived on and collaborated with the Germans., Indeed, if the Germans and the Italians had been wise enough not to invade Greece, Metaxas' state would probably have joined the Axis voluntarily.

But, like most invaders, the Germans were not wise. They made the vast majority of Greeks and even the clergy their enemies. Seizing Greek industry and draining the country of food, they starved the population. Finally, desperate, hungry and angry, a majority of Greeks developed a vigorous anti-Nazi resistance movement.

Even more than Tito's Partisan movement, the Greek National Liberation Front (the EAM) grew into a national movement. The British Secret Intelligence Service (MI6) thought it enrolled virtually the entire adult population and estimated its military force at about 50,000 guerrilla fighters.

We get a sense of what was happening by comparing little Greece to France. While France had a population six times as large as Greece, its anti-Axis resistance probably never numbered more than 1,500 and the part of the French population that collaborated with the Germans was a least half whereas the number of Greeks who did was said to be less than five per cent. And, while the French Underground continuously controlled not a single square mile of land, the EAM controlled almost all of Greece outside the main cities. And German hold on them was effective only sporadically.

As its name indicated, the National Liberation Front (EAM) was determined to come out of the war heading for a new way of life. Finally—like most of the European and Asian liberation movements—it was inspired by and partly led by Communists.

To Churchill, Greek nationalists were just Communists under a different label. In the classical strategic terms in which he was schooled, that meant Greece was under Soviet control. He saw that while the king was with the "lion," the Greek people were with the "bear." Not only would they not block Russian/Soviet moves south, which he regarded as essential for Britain's survival as an empire, but they would be, as South Africa's influential General Smuts was warning, the first "domino" to fall in the "wave of disorder and wholesale communism that was sweeping over Europe." If Greece would not block the expected Russian thrust to the south, Churchill decided Britain must do the job itself.

So Churchill, with his eye fixed on imperial strategy, took an initiative that shaped much of the world in which we have lived during my lifetime. It shaped America's world strategy, but it is still not fully appreciated. So, I will briefly recount it here.

*   *   *

The surest way to "regime change" the EAM, Churchill believed, was military force. And the only available military force was the one General Eisenhower was readying for an attack on German-dominated Europe.

Churchill almost broke up the Anglo-American alliance trying to get the Allied war planners to redirect it from Italy to Greece, but General Eisenhower, then commander of the Anglo-American invasion force, backed by President Roosevelt, refused. In the view of the Anglo-American planners, an attack on Nazi Germany through Greece would have been a costly and perhaps even fatal diversion.

Rebuffed, Churchill decided on another strategy. Since he thought that the Greek EAM was just a Communist organization, he concluded that it must be under the control of Stalin. So, if Eisenhower wouldn't play ball, the game had to be played with Stalin.

In May 1944, Churchill sent Foreign Minister Anthony Eden to Moscow to sound out the Russians. When they seemed receptive to some sort of deal, Churchill himself flew to Moscow in October.

Sitting across the table from Stalin in the Kremlin, he scribbled a short note which he passed over to Stalin. In the note, Churchill proposed a swap: Britain would recognize Soviet post-war control over virtually all of eastern Europe if the Soviet Union would recognize British control of Greece. Stalin, whose relations with the Greek nationalist movement were distant at best and who had no compelling interest in Greece, snapped up the offer.

So it is from Churchill's deal that the Soviet hegemony over eastern Europe may be dated .

Parenthetically, I should also point out that Churchill made his deal almost a year before the Yalta Conference for which Roosevelt was excoriated for having been "soft on Communism" and for having been outsmarted by Stalin. The fact is that it was the great cold warrior, Churchill himself, who planted the corner post of the Iron Curtain. The iron curtain was then hammered into place by the Soviet army's destruction of the German army.

Profiting from the collapse of the German occupation of Greece, Churchill then diverted such troops as he could pull together and which had not been committed to the Italian campaign to invade Greece. Once there, they divided and weakened the Underground and re-imposed the monarchy.

Keeping his part of the bargain, Stalin told the EAM leaders that they had better make a deal with the British— the USSR would not help them.

The EAM tried to fight on. Defeating them proved to be expensive and Britain was nearly broke. It was no longer able to afford Churchill's strategy.

So, with a remarkable sense of resilience and shrewdness, the British Lion turned to the American Eagle.

Only by knowing these events can we understand both the European Cold War and American intervention in Africa and Asia. They are the bed rock of the postwar world in which we continue to live.

*　*　*

Looking back, one is tempted to ask why did America agree to pick up the failed British policy? After all, America had no Indian empire to protect, and it felt secure in holding onto its share of Middle Eastern oil. So the answer must be sought elsewhere. The British shrewdly grasped that the mighty American eagle had a weakness that could be exploited. While it emerged from the war far stronger than the Russian bear, it both exaggerated the capability of the bear and doubted its own prowess.

To win its cooperation, Britain had to play on these attributes. With a new eloquence, Churchill sounded a persuasive message.

Indeed, Churchill's themes were already circulating among the public and its leaders: first among them was fear of Communist subversion. That fear had colored America's view of the world since the 1917 Russian Revolution and was amplified by the perception of domestic social unrest during the Great Depression. Events in Europe., byproducts of the determination not to return to the prewar order, lent credence to domestic fears. And those fears were popularized by religious fundamentalists' crusade against "Godless Communism." Finally came the charge that the American public and foreign nations were too weak, too ignorant of danger and too leaderless to control their own fate. Salvation had to be done for them. Only the American Eagle had the skill, the wealth and the power.

That was the message Mr. Churchill brought to a still very unsophisticated President Truman.

The "fit" was perfect. American leaders had feared Communism domestically for decades, so convincing them of the danger was easy, and the domino image was visually dramatic. It seemed both to explain the war-shattered European states and the loosely-organized colonial areas and to point toward ways to secure them. Above all it had the great virtue of simplicity.

Suddenly, dominos became everyone's favorite game. Image became policy. There was little need to analyze complex events or to know history; it was all simple. If the Bear hit the domino closest to him, the whole row of European states would fall down. Then America would face the same danger that King George identified for Britain: it would lose its place in the world.

That was the fear that l Truman's closest advisers and set the main lines of American policy and organization in the immediate postwar years.

Even much later, when he became President, Ronald Reagan adopted the theme. In a memorable pronouncement he proclaimed that if the Russians "weren't engaged in this game of dominos, there wouldn't be any hot spots in the world."

So, how could America deal with a world of dominos?

Fear that the war-weakened Italy and France would fall

under Communist control was the challenge met by various, mainly covert, actions leading to the Marshall Plan in Europe while the Truman Doctrine was proclaimed for the Middle East and south Asia. Weak nations were to be strengthened through development programs and shaky governments were to be reinforced if possible or replaced if necessary by clients that would perform as directed. Most of them were former protégées of the British, already in place, already trained and already coöpted.

Meanwhile, in the Pacific, Japan had surrendered. The American government believed that more or less single-handedly it had won the Pacific War, and therefore it was entitled to dictate the peace. So, it signed a peace treaty with Japan on its terms (including the preservation of the role of the emperor) on an American battleship under an American flag without any Soviet participation and established its own administration both in Japan and in that part of Korea it controlled.

Further, it massively—but ultimately ineffectively—supported its anti-Communist Chinese ally, led by Chiang Kai-shek, and aided France, also massively but equally ineffectually, in its attempt to recapture its Indo-Chinese colony. Taking a page out of the British playbook for Greece, America also set about suppressing a left-wing nationalist movement, its wartime ally, the Philippine Underground that seemed to Americans an Oriental EAM. Only in Indonesia, did it prevent the reimposition of colonial rule and that only slowly and grudgingly.

Most powerfully it also carried out a coup d'état in Iran in 1953 at the behest of Britain. Britain was determined to hang on to its access to cheap Iranian oil and was treating Iran as a virtual colony. When Iranians installed their first democratically elected government, Britain persuaded America to overthrow it.

Lurking behind all of these diverse and little understood movements were assumed to be local Communists who were the agents of Soviet imperialism. Truman and his advisers, with much encouragement from the British, thought they had to move massively into the chaos and confusion of the post-war and post-colonial worlds. If they did not, they believed, country after country would tumble like dominos and America would find itself virtually alone.

* * *

To cope with this new world, President Truman concluded, America would have to reorganize itself.

Part of the model for a revamped government already existed. The tasks of mobilizing, deploying and sustaining a huge military force, gathering the necessary raw materials and organizing the industry to fabricate weapons and tools had forced the creation of a vast new bureaucracy. Recondite skills had been improved or acquired. Intelligence, both in the sense of acquisition of information and especially code breaking was already well advanced, and the British added to American skills. Spying, what is politely known as "human intelligence," was avidly studied at the feet of the British Secret Intelligence Service (SIS or MI6) by the American OSS. Enough remained of the prewar Army and Navy command structure that it was able to carry the weight of expansion.

But, President Truman and his advisers thought that these early activities had to be regularized and expanded. Thus, in July 1947 at his urging, the Congress passed the National Security Act.

The National Security Act created both the Central Intelligence Agency (the CIA) as the successor to the wartime OSS and the National Security Council (the NSC) and reorganized both the civilian-led departments of the armed forces and centralized their command structure as the Joint Chiefs of Staff., the JCS.

These were the first steps toward what came to known as the "National Security State."

The NSC would preëmpt some of the traditional functions of the Cabinet. Under the chairmanship of the President, originally organized it included the civilian secretaries of Defense, Army, Navy and Air Force, but 2 years later, they were replaced by the general who was chairman of the Joint Chiefs of Staff. Much of the NSC personnel was then and later drawn from the reconstituted intelligence organization, the CIA. As it evolved under President Eisenhower, the NSC became a sort of executive government within the traditional civil government.

Parallel to the NSC and, in some ways to the CIA, was another new organization, the Policy Planning Staff.

When General George Marshall became Secretary of State in 1947, he was appalled to find that the civilian side of the government had no general staff. So, he created the Policy Planning Staff to lay out the master plan on how to deal with the world at large and particularly the Soviet Union. It was this task that brought to the fore two particularly remarkable Americans, George Kennan and Paul Nitze.

*   *   *

Kennan's and Nitze's views of the world and the tasks before the American government were different but different mainly in degree rather than in overall strategy. Both were "hawks," and both focused on the Soviet Union, but Kennan believed that time was on the side of America and that, if handled intelligently, the Soviet Union would evolve peacefully whereas Nitze thought the West had no time. He advocated swift action against what he considered, an evil and implacable enemy.

As Kennan summed up his position, "the Soviet leadership had no preconceived design for world conquest. Its psychology was primarily defensive." But, he also believed that the Soviet Union must be confronted by an impenetrable barrier. That barrier had to be a resurrected Europe anchored on Germany. This he underwrote in the great program he conceived—the Marshall Plan—and embodied it in the concept of Containment.

As I have said, Kennan was no "dove." At that time, there were practically no "doves" roosting in the White House or the State Department and certainly none in the Defense Department. Kennan not only favored the use of power, but he also advocated using all its forms—including espionage—except large-scale armed force. He realized that the clash of armies could not be limited and would return the world to general war. Thus, it would destroy all hopes for well-being, security and peace.

A wise strategy, he argued, was to give the USSR time to evolve toward peace and prosperity while at the same time showing its leaders that aggressive action did not work. That is what he meant by containment.

Behind Kennan's analysis, there were hard facts—even to a layman, it was obvious that Russia had been severely weakened by the German invasion and had not recovered. Close observers reported that in 1947 the US produced 4 times the amount of steel, 5 times the amount of aluminum, 6 times the kwh of power and 8 times the amount of oil as the Soviet Union. And, the gap was widening in America's favor.

Carefully played out, Kennan believed, Containment would force the Soviet leaders to realize that since the costs of war were so horrible and the advantages of America over the Soviet Union were so great the Soviet leaders and their administration would "mellow" or even "converge." Time, he argued, was on the American side.

That was not the conclusion of Paul Nitze.

Nitze was Kennan's successor as director of the Policy Planning Staff. He set out his argument in what was perhaps the most influential government policy paper ever confirmed, NSC-68.

NSC-68, which was commissioned by President Truman on January 1, 1950 and promulgated four months later, called for a massive buildup of both conventional and nuclear arms. In it, Nitze deprecated Kennan's idea of containment. As he wrote, "Without superior aggregate military strength, in being and readily mobilizable, a policy of 'containment'—which is in effect a policy of calculated and gradual coercion—is no more than a policy of bluff."

As McGeorge Bundy commented when he delivered the Henry L Stimson lectures 15 years ago, "NSC-68 took the gloomiest possible view" of détente. Indeed, Nitze's plan called for America to prepare for war. Security would be achieved by overwhelming armed force. And that force would be created by the reorganization not just of the structure of government, but of the whole of the American society and economy. It was, indeed, the origin of what Truman's immediate successor, Dwight Eisenhower was to call the "Military-Industrial Complex."

Nitze's and Kennan's contrasting positions were never seriously debated, even inside the Government, because on June 25, 1950, North Korean military forces crossed the 38th parallel and invaded South Korea. As Secretary of State Dean Acheson later remarked, Korea preëmpted discussion on American strategy. The North Korean action was taken as confirmation of Nitze's argument. NSC-68 became American policy. It has shaped our lives ever since.

More immediately, the hard-fought, nearly-lost and nearly-nuclear Korean war contributed to the climate of fear and mutual distrust so evident among American as they discussed foreign affairs and to the decline of mutual respect and civility within American political circles.

Perhaps more important was the economic thrust of NSC-68. Reacting to it, the USSR was augmenting its already vast military potential, America must at least match it. Or so most of the senior government officials believed. At first, few questioned either the timing or the scale of the required American effort and the American arms industry, having lost much of its wartime market and fearing for its very existence, pushed for maximum expenditure.

One of the few leaders who realized the result of such expenditure was the newly elected president and former armed forces leader, Dwight Eisenhower. In a powerful speech on April 16, 1952 he laid out in graphic detail the social costs of NSC-68:

"This world in arms is not spending money alone. It is spending the sweat of its laborers, the genius of its scientists, the hopes of its children. The cost of one modern heavy bomber is this: a modern brick school in more than 30 cities. It is two electric power plants, each serving a town of 60,000 population. It is two fine, fully equipped hospitals. . . This is not a way of life at all, in any true sense. Under the cloud of threatening war, it is humanity hanging from a cross of iron."

But Eisenhower himself was caught up in the mad rush to fill the world with arms He and his administration believed in Paul Nitze's characterization of the Soviet threat and adopted his, rather than Kennan's strategy, for coping with it. This in turn unleashed powerful profit-seeking corporate forces that combined with the ambitious military hierarchy and "politico-military" advisers to enlist the American political system in what became a juggernaut. At the very end of his administration, Eisenhower himself began to fear the vast transformation of America his administration had fostered and allowed to entrench itself. So, in his final address to the American people on January 17, 1961, he warned that, "...we have been compelled to create a permanent armaments industry of vast proportions. Added to this, three and a half million men and women are directly engaged in the defense establishment. We annually spend on military security more than the net income of all United States corporations.

"This conjunction of an immense military establishment and a large arms industry is new in the American experience. The total influence—economic, political, even spiritual—is felt in every city, every State house, every office of the Federal government. We recognize the imperative need for this development. Yet we must not fail to comprehend its grave implications. Our toil, resources and livelihood are all involved; so is the very structure of our society.

"In the councils of government, we must guard against the acquisition of unwarranted influence, whether sought or unsought, by the military-industrial complex. The potential for the disastrous rise of misplaced power exists and will persist."

Indeed, as George Kennan pointed out in subsequent writings, what had begun as a counterpoise to the Soviet Union took on a life of its own. As he wrote, "Were the Soviet Union to sink tomorrow under the waters of the ocean, the American military–industrial complex would have to remain, substantially unchanged, until some other adversary could be invented. Anything else would be an unacceptable shock to the American economy."

As the enormous proportions of this revolution, began to become known, many of the scientists who had worked on the atomic bomb were horrified Einstein spoke for most of the men who had given America overwhelming power when he said, "If I had known they were going to do this, I would have become a shoemaker." He and a number of other leading scientists formed an organization (known for the name of the Nova Scotia farm where its first meeting was held as "Pugwash") and a journal *(The Bulletin of The Atomic Scientists)* to try to slow down or even give up nuclear weapons, but Nitze had set out a world view and a plan in NSC-68 that both the Democrats and the Republicans found not only necessary but popular and lucrative.

In terms of foreign affairs, however, NSC-68 logically provoked a massive Soviet nuclear weapons build-up and so was self-defeating while, ironically, it was also self-confirming: The Soviet Union began building up its potential for war as Nitze had earlier, prematurely, thought it was doing.

* * *

Thirty years of difficult and dangerous relations would follow. During them Europe recovered, but what had come to be called the Cold War nearly exploded into nuclear war.

Then the objective that both Kennan and Nitze had sought came to fruition—but not because of the actions either man had advocated. Nor, indeed, solely because of the transformation of America into a war machine.

What happened were two developments that neither Kennan nor Nitze could have predicted. The first was that the Soviet Union wrecked itself in a decade-long campaign in the 1980s in the Afghan mountains just as America had bogged itself down in the 1960s in Vietnamese jungles. The difference was that, however costly both engagements were, America could afford its while the Soviet Union could not afford theirs.

The second transformation was that when he became the Soviet leader in the late 1980s, Mikhail Gorbachev undertook a program of divesture of central control and granting of virtual autonomy to the Soviet republics. In this process the structure of the Soviet Union gave way. In the current phrase, the Soviet Union imploded.

*   *   *

Both Kennan and Nitze had focused their attention on the Soviet challenge in Europe. We can follow fairly closely how they shaped the Cold War, but there was no comparable strategist on what the French scholar Alfred Sauvy dubbed *Le Tiers Monde*, "the Third World," the countries of Africa and Asia.

What came to be called The Truman Doctrine was not a new strategy but an echo of a British nineteenth-century policy, the "Forward Policy," aimed at protecting India.

In the Forward Policy, the British had sought to block Russian moves southward by creating a sort of notional wall of colonies or subservient regimes from the Mediterranean to the Pacific. Starting in Egypt (whose Suez Canal formed another "choke point" like the Turkish Straits), the British dominated the Persian Gulf, occupied Iran, invaded Afghanistan, set up outposts in Central Asia, organized a covert military assistance program for China, neutralized Tibet and conquered Burma before reaching the anchorage of Singapore.

The essence of this policy, the notional wall, was picked up a century later by John Foster Dulles when he became Secretary of State. He elaborated it by extensions of the European "wall" of NATO into the Asian walls of CENTO, known as the Baghdad Pact (for the Middle East) and SEATO (for Southeast Asia). That was the essence of American strategy in the 1950s.

As implemented by Dulles, the policy questions were: who would authorize them, who would pay for them and who would provide their military force? These questions take us back to the dilemma set out by the Founding Fathers.

*　*　*

The inescapable dilemma is who makes the decisions—the President, the Congress or, in extremis, the American people? As I have shown in my second talk, this was the essential question argued by the delegates to the Constitutional Convention of 1787 and ruled upon by the Supreme Court in 1936. It was approached from different angles by American thinkers after the Second World War.

Kennan and Nitze agreed with one another and with Alexander Hamilton that the people were not qualified to make decisions on the vital issues of war. But, Madison and most of the delegates to the Constitutional Convention insisted that, ignorant or not, the people had to be involved. American thinkers, statesmen and educators have been struggling ever since to bridge this dilemma.

The dilemma was succinctly put by my favorite

American humorist, Will Rogers. As he lampooned us, the Americans, he said, "The problem ain't what people know. It's what people know that just ain't so that's the problem." The public's lack of knowledge was staggering. As that bitter commentator on America, Ambrose Bierce, categorized the American public with a line from the English poet John Keats, "they stood aloof in giant ignorance."

Giant our ignorance was. Surveys showed that one in four Americans did not know that the Earth circles the Sun. Mark Twain joked that "God created war so that Americans would learn geography," but few learned. We are told that, despite of heavy and expensive engagements and the potential mortal danger to them, 88 per cent of young Americans couldn't find Afghanistan on a map, 75 per cent couldn't locate Iran or Israel, and 63 per cent couldn't identify Iraq, it wasn't just "Faroffistan," more than 7 in 10 did not know what the US government said was the reason for the Cold War with the Soviet Union.

It didn't get much better among the "elite." Among the financially most successful private citizens, wealthy donors to successful presidential candidates who were being nominated to represent the United States abroad, few had even a vague notion of the country to which they were to be assigned. Some of them revealed that they did not even where the country was.

Is this just a fault of our times?

No, a reading of our legislative history shows that Founding Father Gouverneur Morris of New York and Pennsylvania was not entirely wrong when he said that one objective of the Constitution was "to save the people from their most dangerous enemy, themselves."

Morris and his colleagues were deeply concerned about potential manipulation of a fickle and ignorant public by tyrants, and they sought to guard the republic structurally. They were not willing to adopt Hamilton's reshaping of America into a monarchy, but they thought they could accomplish the same aim by dividing the decision-making process and by centering the decision to go to war in the branch of government most immediately responsive to public interest, the Congress.

But, the Congress is just the People with all the faults and short-comings the Founding Fathers had identified. Those faults and short-comings are glaringly evident today. The Congress makes little attempt to embody the national interest but is, itself, essentially up for sale or rent as its members assemble the money they think they need to be reelected. Few who have served in government have much respect for either its wisdom or its integrity.

So, an essential problem has continued and has become more acute: how can "the People" be made more capable of identifying their interests and more interested in defending them? These are, indeed, the fundamental questions of democracy They have no final answer. But, as history teaches us, failure to address them often leads to the death of democracy.

Education was not much discussed during the 1787 Convention. The delegates were themselves a small highly cultured elite to which universities contributed few graduates – Harvard 39 a year, Yale 30, Columbia 15 – and most went to the ministry. Universities paid little attention to the humanities, less to social studies and practically none to science or technology. It was not for another generation that serious attention was given to public education.

In the aftermath of the Second World War, more sophisticated attempts to spread general education were launched at Harvard and the University of Chicago. But, laudable though they were, they tended to be restricted to the academic community and to fail to radiate into the public.

Government secrecy, concealment of failures and outright lies, as Senator Frank Church found in the Senate's remarkable 1975-1976 inquiry into the intelligence aspects of foreign affairs, were a big part of the problem. "In a ˇdemocracy," Church said, "you cannot expect the people…to exercise their judgment if the truth is concealed from them."

But, concealment by government was only part of the problem. The public evidently fails to seek information and both the media and our educational system fail to supply it.

For confirmation of this fact, look at the ultimate danger: nuclear war. Few Americans know anything about nuclear weapons, what they would do or how they might be used. That is, bluntly put, what chances do we or our children have to live or how might we die in a shattered world. Successive administrations and the standing bureaucracy both civil and military have done their best to conceal or jigger the odds. Concealment worked in tandem with public apathy.

In meetings with students and members of public discussion groups all over America, I have found that more people could decipher the meaning of labels on cans of beans than could describe the process on which their lives actually depend. I found few who could even imagine the immediate result of a nuclear war although this has always been public information. Nor do many people know how such a dreadful event could happen.

*   *   *

As former Secretary of Defense Robert McNamara described it, here is the American side of how a nuclear war could happen:

"The decision to fire nuclear weapons is entirely in the hands of one person, the President. He is under no legal obligation to consult with the Congress, other elected officials or statutory officials. The decision is his alone... The whole situation seems so bizarre as to be beyond belief. On any given day, as we go about our business, the president is prepared to make a decision within 20 minutes that could launch one of the most devastating weapons in the world...that is what we have lived with for 40 years. With very few changes, this system remains largely intact…"

What McNamara did not say, but anyone who reflects on his own experience will realize, there are times when one's judgment is questionable—he has a headache, had one cocktail too many or has slept badly. During the Cuban Missile Crisis, I was utterly exhausted and I am sure President Kennedy must have been far more exhausted than I. I presume our Soviet counterparts were too. Much later when I met with them, they told me so. It would be against all experience to bet on anyone always being completely in control of his emotions and always being brave enough in the rapid flow of event to be able to call a halt.

We have so far been lucky. We owe more to President Kennedy and Chairman Khrushchev than most of us realize. Had a man like Chairman Mao been in charge of Soviet forces, we might not now be alive. And what was true of him is partly true of all of us.

Our wise old philosopher Benjamin Franklin warned us that while he trusted the first president, George Washington, he could not predict the worth of his successors. Yet, our nuclear system has given Washington's modern successors, good, bad or indifferent, sole control of life or death for us all.

In addition to the sanity or strength of our leaders and the ignorance or inconstancy of the public, two other things should give us pause. The first is that no matter how technically superb any system is, it is bound to have or develop "glitches" or vulnerabilities.

We know that the warning systems created with great care and at vast expense have registered scores, perhaps hundreds, of false alarms. Some of the false alarms have come close to precipitating warfare. And the system is a favorite target for clever but irresponsible, criminal or perhaps mentally unstable hackers. We know that some have already broken into the most highly touted "secure" systems of the Defense Department and even those of the National Security Agency. I think we have to assume that sooner or later hackers will break into the nuclear command and control system too. Then failings which now focus on the president will be beyond recall. For the failures of presidents and hackers, there is no fail-safe.

Less dramatic but probably more significant is a different weakness of the command and control process. It is actions usually take place in a series of steps that frequently point toward confrontation. When step A is taken, step B appears to be a logical next step, and when step B is taken, step C may seem to be almost inevitable. Momentum can easily dominate judgment. And, momentum may dominate the judgment of both parties in a dispute.

A form of momentum, a sequence of events, precipitated the Cuban Missile Crisis. Observers have tended to focus on the immediate action, which we discovered on October 15 with the placing of Soviet missiles in Cuba. My experience in the unfolding of the crisis leads me to believe that this was only the middle phase of the sequence. Rather, the sequence was set in motion by events that occurred months before. The nature of the sequence is generally passed over or not appreciated by analysts so I will briefly clarify it.

Months before October when the Cuban part of the Crisis erupted, the United States had stationed missiles in Turkey that were nuclear armed and aimed at Soviet cities. The missiles, known as "Jupiters," were liquid propelled and so required at least 15 minutes of preparation to be fired. If they were to be used only in response to an already mounted Soviet attack, they would probably have been wiped out on their launching pads before they could be fired. That is, in strategic terms, they were not deterrents but were offensive or first-strike weapons. Thus, they were destabilizing. They were provocative rather than balancing or preventative; they added nothing to our security while threatening that of the USSR.

Realizing this, I urged that they be removed. They were not. The US Air Force command claimed that they were essential to American security. No one else seemed interested because, after all, we had put similar missiles elsewhere near the Soviet area.

The US Air Force had also stationed in Turkey a squadron of 16 F-100 jet fighter-bombers. As I was organizing an interdepartmental task force on Turkey, I visited this base. There, I found that each plane was armed with a one-megaton bomb, that is approximately 50 times the power of the Hiroshima bomb. At all times, day and night, two of the aircraft were on takeoff pads with pilots in the cockpits, motors running, bombs installed and computers programed for Soviet sites. These aircraft could, of course, be used for first strikes but, because at least two could be airborne in less than a minute, they could be considered to be essentially second strike or retaliatory weapons.

It was the Jupiters whose only purpose was to strike first, not the F-100s, that worried the Russians.

Were they right to be worried and were we right to rely on them as part of our security package? I have cited our view. Let us consider the Soviet view:

History has given the Russians a deep and abiding fear of invasion. Not just the French and the Germans but the British and the Americans have pushed armed forces into Russia or Soviet Asia. The Russians would have had to be blind not to regard the stationing of American missiles on their frontier—what they call "near abroad"—as existential threats. Obviously, they did.

They must have realized that the United States, although it has not been invaded so often or so recently, would similarly regard stationing of Soviet missiles in its Latin American "neighborhood."

So, as we know, the Soviets hit upon a strategy to force the removal of the American missiles: it was simply and logically the stationing comparable forces adjacent to the United States.

With remarkable precision, the Soviet military planners duplicated the American disposition. Their missiles were aimed at Washington whereas ours were aimed at Moscow. Both targets were 1,500 miles distant from the missile bases. And their fighter-bombers IL-28s, which were comparable to our F-100, were programed like ours to attack the "soft underbelly" of each country.

At the end of the confrontation, the solution was simply the removal of both missiles and nuclear devices. That was straight-forward, but not, of course, easy to accomplish. We squeaked through. But just barely.

What is often overlooked is that the Cuban Missile Crisis need never have happened.

The missiles we put in Turkey did not add to our security, but they did provoke the Russians to fear for their security. Luckily for the whole world, President Kennedy and Chairman Khrushchev were strong men and resisted the pressure of their "hawks" to plunge us into a catastrophe. For the crucial days of the Crisis, both also proved to be survivors. Both later paid the price of their cool leadership.

*   *   *

At least on his side, President Kennedy got little support from the public. He did not appear to seek it in those crucial first days. He informed the public what he intended to do and why, but he did not ask for public approval or understanding. That was the tone of his speech on the Monday of the crisis week. In short, I would say that he had roughly the same view of "the people" as our Founding Fathers had: the "cause" was their protection, but it had to be done for them by the wise. Even if this Kennedy's attitude on the Monday when he announced the crisis, he realized that he needed a reasonably informed public later to make the agreement that ended the crisis stick. I saw little evidence that the public demanded much information. It is important to see why this was so and also to think how the dangerous deficiency could be addressed. First, the cause of popular ignorance:

Some 20 newspapers, which previously had offered at least some alternative information, had closed down their foreign bureaus. Whole areas of the country were, and remain today, without significant locally-based and locally-respected media. And, the remaining media—mainly television—have largely given themselves over to entertainment rather than reportage or discussion. The experienced reporter was replaced by the attractive "presenter." Content gave way to spectacle. The media are catering to public tastes rather than to public needs.

Small, scattered and out of touch "public affairs" groups tried to inform themselves but it was a struggle for them and they rarely made themselves heard. Politicians rightly judged their weakness and paid them little attention. Their best audience was the occasional teacher in the public school system and there, as I observed, returning veterans sometimes enlivened otherwise dull textbooks.

But there was little appetite for learning about strange lands and distant peoples even among Americans who had only recently lived among them.

Anticipating the danger of not knowing and not caring, a serious effort had been made at the end of te Second World War under the aegis of Roosevelt's former Under Secretary of State Sumner Wells to teach Americans about the outside world. Wells produced an early guidebook, *An Intelligent American's Guide to the Peace* in 1945 and launched the American Foreign Policy Library with such books *The United States and China* by John King Fairbank, *The United States and Japan* by Edwin Reischauer and my *The United States and the Arab World*. They were adopted as texts by universities, all over America.

Other efforts included the Ford Foundation-funded Intercultural Publications series devoted to the history and culture of other lands. Such attractive collections as "Perspective of India" were published separately and as supplements to The Atlantic magazine and reached hundreds of thousands of secondary and college students. Many commercial and university presses followed. And organizations like the Foreign Policy Association organized public affairs groups in places that had no other access to information on public and particularly foreign policy.

One result was the creation of a market in the public, in universities, in government and, above all, in the military for information, linguistic skills and analysis.

University faculties, that had not devoted much attention to the "Third World," began to allow, at first rather grudgingly, the creation of area studies programs. I set up the one at Chicago and helped to set up the one at Harvard. Recognizing that scholars faced special problems in acquiring language skills, in travel abroad and in designing programs, the Ford and Rockefeller Foundations offered selective support.

Then, in 1958 in reaction to the Soviet launching of Sputnik, the Federal Government got involved. The aim of National Defense Education Act, as the title makes clear, was "to meet national defense needs." Profiting from it, a new generation of students set out to learn about other nations and other cultures.

And, universities, always on the outlook for new sources of funds, increased their already heavy dependence on government support. Even the great universities were drawing most of their funds from the Department of Defense as they had been doing in the efforts of build the atomic bomb. Some became virtual adjuncts to government.

In his last message to the American people as president, Eisenhower had warned that "the free university, historically the fountain-head of new ideas and scientific discovery has experienced a revolution in the conduct of research. Partly because of the great costs involved, a government contract becomes, virtually, a substitute for intellectual curiosity." He did not say, but I think it is evident, that what he meant was that intellectual curiosity was now focused increasingly on security affairs rather than on the humanities, social sciences or pure science.

What Eisenhower touched on was only the tip of the iceberg. With Defense Department or CIA backing and often discrete "guidance," scores of "think tanks" were founded. Meanwhile, the military services converted their training programs into virtual universities. And, not to be outdone, the Air Force founded its own lavishly-funded counterpart to the Soviet Academy of Science's Institute of World Economy and International Affairs, the RAND Corporation. Politico-military studies became the rage in universities and colleges across the land.

* * *

Catching the new wave of politico-military studies brought new opportunities for government-paid fellowships, for publication in government-subsidized journals and for academic promotion. And very little background was required. "Game theory" quickly replaced history, sociology and what was left of the humanities.

Thus, while studies of foreign activities grew, the scopes of studies narrowed. Proponents of politico-military studies regarded the attempts at understanding other peoples, their cultures, politics, traditions and even their languages as irrelevant, unnecessary, trivial or even misleading. In their opinion, nothing was to be gained by such studies. Indeed, the "players," almost like dominos, were seen by game theorists as interchangeable.

What counted was not understanding of their national or cultural characters but the effect of power. And power could be, game theorists argued, precisely measured. Since ability to project force was value free and could be measured for all regimes, regardless of other differences, potential conflict need not become actual. All that mattered was precision in measuring. Danger came from miscalculating. Then a regime might be tempted to "punch above its weight." That need not happen in a thoroughly logical world; so the world leadership must be taught to be logical. This line of thinking appealed particularly to mathematicians and economists in the academic world and to the US Air Force.

Paid for by the Air Force and staffed by mathematicians and economists, the RAND Corporation became the very embodiment of the Cold War. Albert Wohlstetter, who coined the phrase, "the delicate balance of terror," was the high priest, and the crusader was Herman Kahn. Louis Menand's summary of Kahn in the June 25, 2005 New Yorker gives the sense not only of Kahn and Wohlstetter but of the mindset of the whole movement. Reviewing Kahn's book, *On Thermonuclear War*, he wrote "Herman Kahn was the heavyweight of the Megadeath Intellectuals, the men who, in the early years of the Cold War, made it their business to think about the unthinkable, and to design the game plan for nuclear war—how to prevent it, or, if it could not be prevented how to win it, or if it could not be won, how to survive it. The collective combat experience of these men was close to nil; their diplomatic experience was smaller... Kahn was a creature of the RAND Corporation, and RAND was a creature of the Air Force."

The "megadeath intellectuals" were not many, but as true believers in what they laid out, undaunted by the implications of their advice and liberally funded by the Air Force to plot and plan, they exercised a considerable, sometimes even decisive, influence on Washington policy makers in administration after administration from Eisenhower's time. They performed, or were thought to be able to perform, analytical or even specialized operational tasks beyond the capacities of the generalists who made up the government bureaucracy.

Recognition of the use of a cadre of informed, "cleared" but irresponsible experts was widely recognized not only in the American government but also in the Soviet government. After the Missile Crisis, when I had left government service, I met some of their Soviet counterparts at the Institute of World Economy and International Affairs of the Academy of Sciences.

On the central issue posed by the Cuban Missile Crisis, I found the advice of both the Russian and American groups to their governments to have been dangerously misleading.

The American politico-military strategists applied their reasoning in a new version of war gaming derived from the German *kriegsspiel*. They put it forward not only to evaluate plans but even, Arthur Schlesinger wrote, as "the governing force in budgetary, weapons and deployment decisions." He went on to say that in them "reality evaporates in the hallucinatory world where strategic theologians calculate how many warheads can be balanced on the head of a pin. Little seems to me," he continued, "more dangerous than the current fantasy of controlled and graduated nuclear war with generals calibrating nuclear escalation like grand masters at the chessboard. Let us not be bamboozled by models. Once the nuclear threshold is breached, the game is over."

In this new syllabus of the war gamers, the aim was to achieve security by a recognition of the inevitability of military superiority. That was the strategic advice of such "cold warriors" or as they thought of themselves politico-military strategists as Thomas Schelling, Henry Kissinger, Albert Wohlstetter and Herman Kahn. They were "warriors from afar." Almost none of them had ever been "in harm's way." For them war was not the horror of combat but the calculation, even the delight, of chess.

As their ideas spread in government circles—the State Department created a new bureau on "politico-military" affairs—and in the academic and quasi-academic community, a new school of international relations "theory" grew around these concepts. The result was not so much a growth of sophistication and capacity in the "public sector," but, as Eisenhower had warned, the coöption of the more ambitious members of the "theory class."

Not only war-making but war-thinking came to be an addiction of the White House and the entire Executive

Branch. Academic and semi-academic research followed the money, and increasingly it came to focus on questions of "how" policies should be carried out rather than "whether or not" they should be. This was a perhaps inevitable consequence of the Cold War.

As I have already discussed, Paul Nitze's NSC-68 gave the president authority to launch wars, including even a nuclear war, if he chooses, without provocation. In sum, our lives are completely and utterly in his hands. What could provoke such a disastrous move? Our lives depend in large part—but in ways that appear obscure to most of us—on what could provoke the operation of the vast and even potentially suicidal power we have given our presidents.

*   *   *

Of course, most of us thought that we must give our presidents this unlimited power. Long before 1983 when President Reagan coined the phrase, the Soviet Union was considered to be the "Evil Empire." In popular as well as governmental estimation, the Soviet Union was determined to destroy us, ruin our way of life and overturn our efforts to create a peaceful, just and prosperous world. So, finding out what the Russians were actually doing had already by 1946 given rise to what became a vast program for surveillance of the USSR and its satellites.

We found it hard to believe, but of course the Russians echoed our view in their view of us. They were sure that we intended to "regime change" their country, to destroy their economy, to disengage their alliances and to break up their Union.

So, both of us believed that we were governed by the imperative of a "need to know." In the technology of that era, this particular need to know had to be addressed largely by aerial surveillance.

At first, an implicit US-USSR "gentleman's agreement" restricted intrusive flights of aircraft to no closer than 40 miles from borders. Soviet planes flew along the Atlantic coast of America and American planes flew along all the frontiers of the Soviet Union. At first, neither side intruded into the territory of the other.

Then in 1949 the Soviet Union exploded its first nuclear device, and in November 1950 Chinese forces entered Korea. On December 16, 1950, President Truman declared a state of National Emergency. Suddenly, gathering intelligence on Soviet capabilities, particularly on the presumed ability of the Soviet air force to attack the United States across Alaska and Canada, became insistent. At the behest of the Air Force and his advisers, Truman immediately approved American aerial penetrations of Siberia.

The US had just acquired a new, relatively fast, high-flying bomber, the B-47, that could be modified for the task. The pilots of the B-47 took the first step in a lengthy game of hide and seek in which both Russian and American fighter planes intercepted, followed, photographed but usually did not shoot down each other's aircraft.

However, surveillance soon turned into provocation. In the spring of 1956, President Eisenhower authorized a major aerial invasion of the Soviet Union. Armed B-47 bombers took off from an American airbase at Thule, Greenland and overflew virtually the whole stretch of the Russian Arctic. As James Bamford has written, "Over seven weeks, almost daily, between eight and ten bombers launched, refueled, over the North Pole, and continued south across the Russian border. In one incursion, six aircraft, flying abreast flaunted American power in broad daylight as though on a nuclear bombing run. Had they not been caught unprepared, the Russians might well have launched a counterattack, with devastating results."

The Soviet military's inability to stop the American flights must have been professionally humiliating. When they could, they reacted. The first armed clash came, apparently (for this information is still restricted) in 1949. In the following eleven years a dozen or more US aircraft were shot down or crashed in or near the USSR.

Neither side admitted that a small-scale and covert war had already broken out. The military commanders and intelligence chiefs on both sides knew exactly what was happening, but at least on the American side even senior civilian officials were denied access to information on the "mishaps."

The public on both sides was kept completely in the dark. But it gradually became clear that the pattern of events would become known and that it was too dangerous to continue. Finally, the CIA ordered a new plane, the

Lockheed jet-powered glider, the U-2, and had it flown by CIA contract pilots. It was CIA contract pilot Gary Powers who flew the U-2 that was brought down over the USSR on May 1, 1960. The shooting down of the U-2 was perhaps the most publicized event of the Cold War.

Fortunately, the advances of rocket technology and high resolution sensing devices have now rendered obsolete what could have been a trigger for war. But, of course, many other potential causes of war were brought into play by the same advance in technology. Today, there are now many more pieces of equipment, vastly more dangerous than the U-2, placed provocatively in sensitive regions throughout the world. The quest for information is endless.

*　　*　　*

Provocations were often senseless and almost always highly dangerous, but, almost as dangerous, were accidents and mistakes. As we all know, when almost anything, even paperclips, run into the thousands, things are almost certain to get lost or get broken. So it has been with nuclear weapons. Despite great and expensive efforts at command and control, there have been a number of near catastrophes. Presumably the Russians have had similar experiences.

It is believed that about 50 American nuclear bombs along with 26 nuclear reactors were lost from 1950 to 1980. What happened after that date is unreported, but it is probably that as many as a thousand significant nuclear bomb accidents, most of which could have wiped out a large city, have occurred.

Former Secretary of Defense William Perry reported one that shows how accidental could be the pulling of the trigger of a nuclear war. The watch officer at the Strategic Air Command called Perry in the middle of the night to report that 200 Russian ICBMs had been picked up on Radar heading for America. Fortunately, the general discovered that the wrong tape had been inserted in the computer. It was a near miss: a response by American missiles or aircraft could have been a real-life enactment of the film Fail Safe which gave us "Dr. Strangelove."

Sometimes even more dangerous than deliberate provocation or accident was routine: During the week of the Cuban Missile Crisis, the American Air Force went ahead with a previously scheduled test of an ICBM. It had previously been programmed; so, despite the fact that we were hovering on the brink of war, those in charge simply went ahead.

While I had access supposedly to all actions during that week, I did not find out about the missile test until later. Remarkably, the Soviet intelligence services do not seem to have discovered it either. Had they done so, they presumably would have regarded it as directed against their forces in Cuba with possibly disastrous results.

One does not have to be paranoid or a believer in conspiracy theories to question whether such near misses are accidental or deliberate. I had ample reason to know that a number of our senior military officers and some senior civilian officials were pushing the President toward war. He was able to resist because no attack eventuated, but had the Russians detected the missile test Secretary Perry described, and reacted, the President almost certainly could not have resisted doing what the generals were trying to force him to do. Mr. Perry, who was closer to the military than I, reached the same conclusion. As he wrote, "many advisors wanted to rush us into war."

One plan to rush us into war was "Operation Northwoods." It was a plan to provoke a war with Cuba by both real and simulated attacks on Americans in which some would be murdered and the public would be told that they had been killed by order of Fidel Castro. Had the plan been implemented, almost certainly, regardless of his policy, the President would have been rushed into war,

The plan was prepared by a secret military unit under the auspices of the chairman of the Joint Chiefs of Staff, General Lyman Lemnitzer. Lemnitzer also attempted to enlist his fellow generals; therefore it is not unlikely that implementation of the plan could have been the opening gun in a *coup d'état*. In effect, preparation for a coup had already begun since the military command was making plans and creating situations beyond the knowledge or control of their civilian superiors, including the President and the Secretary of Defense. Their action was treasonous. But it nearly happened.

While the joint chiefs of staff prevented even the Secretary of Defense from finding out about their activities, they revealed at least part of their plan to the "think tank" of the Air Force, the RAND corporation and there one of the politico-military theoreticians, Daniel Ellsberg, recoiled from the horror of their plan. In his 2017 book, *The Doomsday Machine: Confessions of a Nuclear War Planner,* Ellsberg points out that, if implemented, the related nuclear strikes would have wiped out every city and most towns of the Soviet Union and China, killing about half of the world's population, devastating much of the rest of the world and almost certainly causing a Soviet counterattack that, even with the remnant of the Soviet nuclear force that would have survived the American attack, would have burned to death about half the American population.

* * *

As you will have observed, I have had to leave out many topics in the time we have spent together. I have concentrated on the larger scene of strategy rather than the flow of events. I have not treated in detail here, though I have written on it elsewhere, the changes in our society brought about by the growth of the military-industrial complex and the lamentable and dangerous decline in the standards of civil discussion of national affairs.

Perhaps I can do no better than to leave you with the plea that as each of us reviews the doleful events that daily impinge on our thoughts, we go to the bottom line:—do we feel safer as a result of the policies we have implemented or not? If not, then what could we have learned? And what could be do to get on a safer road?

I am impressed by two sequences of events: time proved to work to our benefit in the Cold War. When we moved further from war with the Soviet Union and got out of Vietnam the process of "healing" was dramatic. We breathed easier and the Vietnamese moved toward a peaceful society.

But we have not applied or continued those successes. Rather, we have gone back to the failed policies of the 1950s in pushing NATO into the Russian security zone and in seeking to overwhelm or forcibly "regime change" societies in the Third World. We have besmirched our own self-image with the application of torture, long-term and brutal imprisonment and even by the assassination of the leaders of other nations. We may turn aside from admitting these events although doing so would difficult since our own government has documented them.

What we cannot do is to hide our actions from relatives and fellow countrymen of the victims. Worse, we have sought to enroll their leaders in our actions and so have corrupted the entire order of world affairs. Unwittingly, we have made our world a far less safe place for ourselves and for almost everyone else.

We have reacted with horror at the actions of those we call terrorists and who think of themselves as freedom fighters or defenders. There is much savagery on both sides of the terrible events that arise from this clash.

I am not qualified to pass moral judgment on these events, but I am trained to evaluate the results: our attempt to achieve security by military, paramilitary, and other means has not worked. Nor is it likely to work. Over the last decades we have given it every chance, have paid out trillions of dollars and the blood of thousands of our young men and women. In the very attempt to achieve greater security, damage to the essence of our political system, our civic culture, and our freedom will certainly grow. The end is not in sight the costs are accumulating. Those who led us astray have not reformed. They are still promoting acts that will harm us all and with harm us to no benefit to our security.

We must ask ourselves: are we on the way, at long last, toward ending what the Founding Fathers thought of as our experiment with democracy? Are we in danger of fulfilling the prophecy of the man the great American historian Henry Adams called New England's "most brilliant writer and talker," Fisher Ames, who in 1803 wrote that "A democracy cannot last. Its nature ordains that its next change shall be into a military Despotism… The reason is that the tyranny of what is called the people, and that by the sword both operate alike to debase and corrupt, till there neither men left with the spirit to desire liberty, or morals with the power to sustain justice."

This is certainly a dire warning and was given a long time ago. I hope and trust that it is wrong, but I leave you with the judgment of our great teacher, Benjamin Franklin. He warned, "Those who would give up essential liberty to purchase a little temporary safety, deserve neither liberty nor safety."

Will we, can we, accept his warning?

William R. Polk, BA & MA (Oxford) BA & PhD (Harvard) was born in Texas and grew up on a ranch. After graduating from Harvard University he was awarded a Rockefeller Foundation fellowship for studies in the Middle East.

During two years of research he wrote a "Headline Series" booklet for the Foreign Policy Association, edited an edition of The Atlantic and studied at the University of Baghdad and the American University of Beirut. Then also as a Rockefeller Foundation fellow he read Oriental Studies at Oxford. In 1955, he returned to Harvard as the assistant to Professor Sir Hamilton Gibb, then the world's outstanding Orientalist, , and helped establish the University's Center for Middle Eastern Studies, While getting his doctorate, he taught a post- graduate seminar on Arabic historiography.

During that time, together with Richard Nolte, an Oxford colleague then at the Institute of Current World Affairs, who later was the American ambassador to Egypt, he wrote an article on the failure of American Middle Eastern policy. That article in Foreign Affairs caused Governor Chester Bowles, then Under Secretary of State and McGeorge Bundy, then Director of the National Security Council, to urge President Kennedy to appoint him as the Member of the Policy

Planning Council, responsible for North Africa, the Middle East and West Asia.

In that capacity, he served for 4 years under Presidents Kennedy and Johnson, During that time he was a member of the three-men Crisis Management Committee during the Cuban Missile Crisis and head of the interdepartmental task force that helped to end the Franco-Algerian war. He prepared U.S. National Policy documents on Turkey, Egypt, Afghanistan and on the Palestine issue.

Largely over his opposition to the Vietnam war policy, he resigned in 1965 to become Professor of History at the University of Chicago. He was the founding director of the University's Middle Eastern Studies Center and a founder and member of the board of directors of the American Middle Eastern Studies Association.

He then founded and became President of the Adlai Stevenson Institute of International Affairs, among whose fellows were former UN Secretary General U Thant, British Ambassador to the UN Lord Caradon; the soon to be Prime Minister of Russia Evgeny Primakov, former Deputy Prime Minister of Afghanistan Abdel Keyyum, former Foreign Minister of Ghana Fred Arkhurst, director of the UN Environment Program and Mayor of Bogota Enrique Peñalosa, former Deputy Director of the Bureau of the Budget Kenneth Hansen and former Deputy Editor of The Economist Lady Jackson (Barbara Ward) as well as the journalists David Halberstam, Murray Kempton and Neil Sheehan, each of whom wrote his major works at the Institute.

During this time, at the request of Israeli Prime Minister Golda Meir, he negotiated with President Gamal Abdul Nasser the ceasefire that ended Israeli-Egyptian fighting on the Suez Canal in 1970.

He is the author of some 17 books on world affairs, including The United States and the Arab World; The Elusive Peace, the Middle East in the Twentieth Century; Understanding Iraq; Out of Iraq (with Senator George McGovern); Understanding Iran; Violent Politics: A History of Insurgency and Terrorism; Neighbors and Strangers: The Fundamentals of Foreign Affairs; Humpty Dumpty: The Fate of Regime Change; and Distant Thunder: Reflections on the Dangers of Our Times. And just published by the Yale University Press in January 2018, Crusade and Jihad: The Thousand-Year War Between The Muslim World and the Global North. Reviews of his books can be accessed on his website, www.williampolk.com.

Numbers of his articles have appeared in Foreign Affairs, The Atlantic, Harpers, The Bulletin of the Atomic Scientists and Le Monde Diplomatique.

Mr. Polk has lectured at many universities and at the Council on Foreign Relations, Chatham House, Sciences Po, the Soviet Academy of Sciences' Institute of World Economy and International Affairs and has appeared frequently on NPR, the BBC, CBS, France 24 and other networks. He was recently appointed Visiting Distinguished Professor at Sciences Po and named Nonresident Senior Fellow of the Center for International Policy. He has been awarded 4 Rockefeller Foundation Fellowships and 1 Guggenheim fellowship.

Among his recent essays are "The Struggle for Palestine," "The Russian view of the Ukrainian Crisis," "Understanding Syria," "the Danger of War with Iran," "the Sense of Drift and Disorder in World Affairs" and "Toward a National Strategy to Deal with a New World."

He and Prime Minister Evgeny Primakov of Russia had begun a joint autobiography that was to be entitled Parallel Lives showing how they had reached across the barriers of the Cold War in search of peace. It was terminated by Primakov's death.

He is now at work on a history and critique of the concept of Strategy.

He has four children and is married to Baroness Elisabeth von Oppenheimer.